# ingenious BRILLIANT LOGIC PUZZLES

## BEN ADDLER

SIRIUS

**SIRIUS**

This edition published in 2019 by Sirius Publishing, a division of
Arcturus Publishing Limited,
26/27 Bickels Yard, 151–153 Bermondsey Street,
London SE1 3HA

Copyright © Arcturus Holdings Limited
Puzzles copyright © Puzzle Press Ltd

ISBN: 978-1-78950-724-9
AD007394NT

Printed in China

# CONTENTS

# HOW TO SOLVE A LOGIC PUZZLE

Never tried a logic puzzle before? Don't worry! It's really not that hard. All you need is patience and a methodical approach, to sort out the positive and negative information you are given. All the relevant facts are there on the page in front of you.

Let's take things step by step. To make identification easier for complete beginners, we've lettered the squares of the grid in this example.

Three children each have different last names and different hair shades. Which is which?

1. The redhead whose last name is Dale isn't Bill.
2. Colin (whose hair is brown) isn't the child named Lake.

|  | Last name | | | Hair | | |
|---|---|---|---|---|---|---|
|  | Dale | Hill | Lake | Black | Brown | Red |
| Amy | A | B | C | D | E | F |
| Bill | G | H | I | J | K | L |
| Colin | M | N | O | P | Q | R |
| Black | S | T | U |  |  |  |
| Brown | V | W | X |  |  |  |
| Red | Y | Z | Ω |  |  |  |

| Child | Last name | Hair |
|---|---|---|
| AMY | DALE | RED |
|  |  |  |
|  |  |  |

Start filling the grid, using crosses for the negative, and checks for the positive information in the clues.

Clue 1 states that the redhead is named Dale, so put a check in square Y, and crosses in squares S, V, Z, and Ω. Clue 1 also states that Bill isn't the redhead, so put a cross in square L. Thus since Bill isn't Dale, put a cross in square G. Your grid now looks like this:

|  | Last name | | | Hair | | |
|---|---|---|---|---|---|---|
|  | Dale | Hill | Lake | Black | Brown | Red |
| Amy |  |  |  |  |  |  |
| Bill | X |  |  |  |  | X |
| Colin |  |  |  |  |  |  |
| Black | X |  |  |  |  |  |
| Brown | X |  |  |  |  |  |
| Red | ✓ | X | X |  |  |  |

Clue 2 states that Colin has brown hair, so put a check in square Q and crosses in squares P, R, E, and K. Your grid now looks like this:

|  | Last name | | | Hair | | |
|---|---|---|---|---|---|---|
|  | Dale | Hill | Lake | Black | Brown | Red |
| Amy |  |  |  |  | X |  |
| Bill | X |  |  |  | X | X |
| Colin |  |  |  | X | ✓ | X |
| Black | X |  |  |  |  |  |
| Brown | X |  |  |  |  |  |
| Red | ✓ | X | X |  |  |  |

Since there are crosses in both squares K and L, the only possibility remaining for Bill's hair shade is black; so you can put a check into square J, and a cross in square D.

The child with red hair is thus Amy, so put a check in square F. Since the red-haired child is named Dale (clue 1), you can put a check in square A, and crosses in squares B, C, and M.

The child named Lake isn't Colin (clue 2), so Bill; thus you can put a check in square I, and crosses in squares H and O.

Since Colin has brown hair, you can put a cross in square X, and thus a check in W. The child named Hill is thus Colin, so put a check in square N.

Now you can fill the solution box with the details.

Your finished grid and solution box now look like this:

|  | Last name | | | Hair | | |
|---|---|---|---|---|---|---|
|  | Dale | Hill | Lake | Black | Brown | Red |
| Amy | ✓ | X | X | X | X | ✓ |
| Bill | X | X | ✓ | ✓ | X | X |
| Colin | X | ✓ | X | X | ✓ | X |
| Black | X | X | ✓ |  |  |  |
| Brown | X | ✓ | X |  |  |  |
| Red | ✓ | X | X |  |  |  |

| Child | Last name | Hair |
|---|---|---|
| Amy | Dale | Red |
| Bill | Lake | Black |
| Colin | Hill | Brown |

# Head Girls

St Margharete's College is a school for the daughters of the very rich (as is reflected in the fees it charges!). At the start of every scholastic year in the second week of September, pupils vote for a new Head Girl. Study the clues below to arrive at the first name and last name of each Head Girl in the given years.

1  There were exactly two other Head Girls between Clarice's term of office and that of Miss Palmer.

2  Davina was appointed Head Girl in an earlier year than Miss Woods, who was appointed two years before Miss Mickel's unopposed election to the position.

3  Elaine's last name is Dale.

4  Miss Ambridge was elected to serve during the 2004/2005 school year, but didn't succeed Marian.

|  | First name | | | | | Last name | | | | |
|---|---|---|---|---|---|---|---|---|---|---|
|  | Clarice | Davina | Elaine | Marian | Venetia | Ambridge | Dale | Mickel | Palmer | Woods |
| 2002/2003 | | | | | | | | | | |
| 2003/2004 | | | | | | | | | | |
| 2004/2005 | | | | | | | | | | |
| 2005/2006 | | | | | | | | | | |
| 2006/2007 | | | | | | | | | | |
| Ambridge | | | | | | | | | | |
| Dale | | | | | | | | | | |
| Mickel | | | | | | | | | | |
| Palmer | | | | | | | | | | |
| Woods | | | | | | | | | | |

| Years | First name | Last name |
|---|---|---|
| | | |
| | | |
| | | |
| | | |
| | | |

# Souvenirs

Liam is on a plane, going home from a two-week holiday in Spain. Before he left the airport, he used up his remaining currency (euros) to buy a souvenir gift for each of the members of his family, choosing the items from five different shops in the duty free area. Can you discover the order in which he purchased each item, together with the family member to whom it will be given?

1 Liam bought the castanets earlier than (but not immediately before) he purchased a present (not sherry) for his aunt.

2 Liam's aunt's present was bought earlier than the gift for his cousin.

3 The second gift purchased by Liam wasn't that for his mother, which was purchased either immediately before or immediately after the sombrero.

4 The gift of a cigar box for his brother was bought immediately after the bottle of Rioja red wine.

|  | Order | | | | | Gift for | | | | |
|---|---|---|---|---|---|---|---|---|---|---|
|  | First | Second | Third | Fourth | Fifth | Aunt | Brother | Cousin | Father | Mother |
| Castanets |  |  |  |  |  |  |  |  |  |  |
| Cigar box |  |  |  |  |  |  |  |  |  |  |
| Red wine |  |  |  |  |  |  |  |  |  |  |
| Sherry |  |  |  |  |  |  |  |  |  |  |
| Sombrero |  |  |  |  |  |  |  |  |  |  |
| Aunt |  |  |  |  |  |
| Brother |  |  |  |  |  |
| Cousin |  |  |  |  |  |
| Father |  |  |  |  |  |
| Mother |  |  |  |  |  |

| Gift | Order | Gift for |
|---|---|---|
|  |  |  |
|  |  |  |
|  |  |  |
|  |  |  |
|  |  |  |

# Charity Donations

Four members of the same family each gave an amount of money to a different charity last week. How much did each donate, on which day, and in what field does each person's chosen organization work?

1 The charity working with elderly people received more money than was given by Lou, but less money than was donated on Wednesday.

2 The charity working to find homes for unwanted domestic animals received less money than was donated by Chris, but more than was given by Annie.

3 The sum of twenty dollars was given the day before a donation was made to the charity concerned with the relief of famine.

|  | Amount | | | | Day | | | | Field | | | |
|---|---|---|---|---|---|---|---|---|---|---|---|---|
|  | $20 | $25 | $30 | $35 | Monday | Wednesday | Thursday | Friday | Animals | Children | Elderly | Famine |
| Annie |  |  |  |  |  |  |  |  |  |  |  |  |
| Chris |  |  |  |  |  |  |  |  |  |  |  |  |
| Lou |  |  |  |  |  |  |  |  |  |  |  |  |
| Tony |  |  |  |  |  |  |  |  |  |  |  |  |
| Animals |  |  |  |  |  |  |  |  |
| Children |  |  |  |  |  |  |  |  |
| Elderly |  |  |  |  |  |  |  |  |
| Famine |  |  |  |  |  |  |  |  |
| Monday |  |  |  |  |
| Wednesday |  |  |  |  |
| Thursday |  |  |  |  |
| Friday |  |  |  |  |

| Name | Amount | Day | Field |
|---|---|---|---|
|  |  |  |  |
|  |  |  |  |
|  |  |  |  |
|  |  |  |  |

**4**

# Wedding Bells

Mrs Robins' four granddaughters all married in different months last year and are about to provide her with four great-grandchildren. Can you discover the first name and last name of the man each married, together with the month in which they were wed?

1 Of the four granddaughters: one is Denise; one married Bobby; one is Mrs Unwin; and one was married in January.

2 Of the four granddaughters: one is Edith; one married Roger; one is Mrs Danish; and one was married three months after Mrs Danish.

3 Of the four granddaughters: one is Julia; one married Philip; one is Mrs Court; and one (not Mrs Matthews) was married in July.

4 Of the four granddaughters: one is Stephanie; one married Andrew; one is Mrs Matthews; and one married three months after Mrs Matthews.

5 Of the four granddaughters: one is Edith; one married Andrew; one is Mrs Court; and one married three months after Mrs Court.

|  | Andrew | Bobby | Philip | Roger | Court | Danish | Matthews | Unwin | January | April | July | October |
|---|---|---|---|---|---|---|---|---|---|---|---|---|
| Denise |  |  |  |  |  |  |  |  |  |  |  |  |
| Edith |  |  |  |  |  |  |  |  |  |  |  |  |
| Julia |  |  |  |  |  |  |  |  |  |  |  |  |
| Stephanie |  |  |  |  |  |  |  |  |  |  |  |  |
| January |  |  |  |  |  |  |  |  |
| April |  |  |  |  |  |  |  |  |
| July |  |  |  |  |  |  |  |  |
| October |  |  |  |  |  |  |  |  |
| Court |  |  |  |  |
| Danish |  |  |  |  |
| Matthews |  |  |  |  |
| Unwin |  |  |  |  |

| Name | Husband | Last name | Month |
|---|---|---|---|
|  |  |  |  |
|  |  |  |  |
|  |  |  |  |
|  |  |  |  |

8

# Top Dogs

The first five prizes in the local dog show were awarded to those dogs and owners who appear in this puzzle. Can you work out the facts, in terms of the name of the dog which won each listed prize, as well as that of the proud owner?

1 Butch was awarded a prize either one place higher or one place lower than that won by the dog belonging to Miss Barnes.

2 Mr Allen's dog achieved a position more than one place higher than that awarded to Nero and his owner.

3 Third prize didn't go to Mrs Fletcher's dog. Mrs Fletcher's dog achieved a higher placing than Sam.

4 Neither Mrs Fletcher nor Mrs Morris owns Butch. Mrs Morris' dog achieved a prize more than one place higher than that awarded to Mrs Fletcher's dog.

5 Mr Yates's dog was placed either two higher or two lower than Fido.

|  | Butch | Chester | Fido | Nero | Sam | Mr Allen | Miss Barnes | Mrs Fletcher | Mrs Morris | Mr Yates |
|---|---|---|---|---|---|---|---|---|---|---|
| First prize |  |  |  |  |  |  |  |  |  |  |
| Second prize |  |  |  |  |  |  |  |  |  |  |
| Third prize |  |  |  |  |  |  |  |  |  |  |
| Fourth prize |  |  |  |  |  |  |  |  |  |  |
| Fifth prize |  |  |  |  |  |  |  |  |  |  |
| Mr Allen |  |  |  |  |  |
| Miss Barnes |  |  |  |  |  |
| Mrs Fletcher |  |  |  |  |  |
| Mrs Morris |  |  |  |  |  |
| Mr Yates |  |  |  |  |  |

| Prize | Dog | Owner |
|---|---|---|
|  |  |  |
|  |  |  |
|  |  |  |
|  |  |  |
|  |  |  |

# Boys' Toys

Each of the boys in this puzzle had his heart set on a small, inexpensive toy, but none had any money. The boys therefore did small jobs around their homes, in return for payment, until each had saved enough to buy what he wanted. What task did each boy undertake, and what did he buy?

1  Douglas saved enough to buy a toy helicopter with rotating blades.

2  The boy who saved to buy a ship to play with in the bath washed windows, unlike Grant.

3  Harry (who didn't buy the kite) did the dishes each evening after dinner, and Ewan vacuumed the carpets in order to earn money.

4  One boy bought a shiny red sports car with the money he earned from dusting furniture around the house.

|  | Task | | | | | Toy | | | | |
|---|---|---|---|---|---|---|---|---|---|---|
|  | Dishes | Dusting | Gardening | Vacuuming | Windows | Car | Helicopter | Kite | Ship | Spinning top |
| Douglas |  |  |  |  |  |  |  |  |  |  |
| Ewan |  |  |  |  |  |  |  |  |  |  |
| Grant |  |  |  |  |  |  |  |  |  |  |
| Harry |  |  |  |  |  |  |  |  |  |  |
| Lenny |  |  |  |  |  |  |  |  |  |  |
| Car |  |  |  |  |  |  |  |  |  |  |
| Helicopter |  |  |  |  |  |  |  |  |  |  |
| Kite |  |  |  |  |  |  |  |  |  |  |
| Ship |  |  |  |  |  |  |  |  |  |  |
| Spinning top |  |  |  |  |  |  |  |  |  |  |

| Boy | Task | Toy |
|---|---|---|
|  |  |  |
|  |  |  |
|  |  |  |
|  |  |  |
|  |  |  |

# Dress Design

The new ladies' fashion store in town has an exciting display of rather over-priced dresses, each by a different designer. Study the clues and the diagram of the display to discover not only the name of the designer of each, but also its shade, and price tag.

1 The dress designed especially by Delacci costs less than the one immediately next to and left of the red dress (which wasn't designed by Delacci).
2 Dress C is white and is immediately between the dress designed by Dovetti and the one with the $3,250 price tag.
3 The dress designed by Ducanno is further left than the beige dress.
4 The black dress is priced at $3,000.
5 Dyablo's dress isn't the one with the most expensive price tag.

|  | Designer | | | | Shade | | | | Price | | | |
|---|---|---|---|---|---|---|---|---|---|---|---|---|
|  | Delacci | Dovetti | Ducanno | Dyablo | Beige | Black | Red | White | $3,000 | $3,250 | $3,500 | $4,000 |
| Dress A | | | | | | | | | | | | |
| Dress B | | | | | | | | | | | | |
| Dress C | | | | | | | | | | | | |
| Dress D | | | | | | | | | | | | |
| $3,000 | | | | | | | | | | | | |
| $3,250 | | | | | | | | | | | | |
| $3,500 | | | | | | | | | | | | |
| $4,000 | | | | | | | | | | | | |
| Beige | | | | | | | | | | | | |
| Black | | | | | | | | | | | | |
| Red | | | | | | | | | | | | |
| White | | | | | | | | | | | | |

LEFT ⇦          RIGHT ⇨

A   B   C   D

| Dress | Designer | Shade | Price |
|---|---|---|---|
| | | | |
| | | | |
| | | | |
| | | | |

# Ships That Pass…

… in the night. Roger Jolly is a retired seaman who walks his dog along the cliff path every evening. Roger always takes a pair of binoculars with him, as he likes to keep a lookout for passing ships. He spotted four last night, and if you study the clues below, you can discover details of each including its type, the city in which it is registered, and details of its hull.

1 The freighter and the vessel with a green hull both have names of the same length.

2 The tanker (which has a blue hull) wasn't registered in Monrovia (which is the capital of Liberia). The tanker isn't the *Carolyn*, which was registered in London.

3 The cruise liner has a white hull.

4 The *Trivorn* was registered in Hamburg.

5 The vessel with a green hull was registered in Panama City. It isn't the *Barbel*.

|  | Type | | | | City | | | | Hull | | | |
|---|---|---|---|---|---|---|---|---|---|---|---|---|
|  | Freighter | Liner | Tanker | Tug | Hamburg | London | Monrovia | Panama City | Black | Blue | Green | White |
| Barbel |  |  |  |  |  |  |  |  |  |  |  |  |
| Carolyn |  |  |  |  |  |  |  |  |  |  |  |  |
| Hotari |  |  |  |  |  |  |  |  |  |  |  |  |
| Trivorn |  |  |  |  |  |  |  |  |  |  |  |  |
| Black |  |  |  |  |  |  |  |  |
| Blue |  |  |  |  |  |  |  |  |
| Green |  |  |  |  |  |  |  |  |
| White |  |  |  |  |  |  |  |  |
| Hamburg |  |  |  |  |
| London |  |  |  |  |
| Monrovia |  |  |  |  |
| Panama City |  |  |  |  |

| Ship | Type | City | Hull |
|---|---|---|---|
|  |  |  |  |
|  |  |  |  |
|  |  |  |  |
|  |  |  |  |

# Two-Course Meals

A new restaurant opened in town last month, and five friends ate there on the 27th, each choosing a different first and second course. Discover what everyone ate by studying the clues below.

1 Fergus isn't the man who ate both chicken pie and strawberry pavlova.

2 Rosie is the sister of the person who chose a juicy venison steak followed by lemon cheesecake.

3 The person who tucked into tiramisu didn't choose lasagne as a first course.

4 Sarah ate a mild beef curry, but not tiramisu.

5 David chose the apple pie.

|  | 1st Course | | | | | 2nd Course | | | | |
|---|---|---|---|---|---|---|---|---|---|---|
|  | Beef curry | Chicken pie | Lamb's liver | Lasagne | Venison | Apple pie | Cheesecake | Ice cream | Pavlova | Tiramisu |
| David |  |  |  |  |  |  |  |  |  |  |
| Fergus |  |  |  |  |  |  |  |  |  |  |
| Rosie |  |  |  |  |  |  |  |  |  |  |
| Sarah |  |  |  |  |  |  |  |  |  |  |
| Timothy |  |  |  |  |  |  |  |  |  |  |
| Apple pie |  |  |  |  |  |
| Cheesecake |  |  |  |  |  |
| Ice cream |  |  |  |  |  |
| Pavlova |  |  |  |  |  |
| Tiramisu |  |  |  |  |  |

| Diner | 1st | 2nd |
|---|---|---|
|  |  |  |
|  |  |  |
|  |  |  |
|  |  |  |
|  |  |  |

# Safe and Sound

Five customers of Harkley's Bank each have a safety
deposit box containing a personal item which belonged
to a (now deceased) relative. Can you discover the
contents of each person's safety deposit box, together
with the person to whom the item used to belong?

**1** Claire isn't the woman who keeps her grandmother's diamond
brooch safely locked away.

**2** Mike keeps an item which used to belong to his father; it isn't a
painting.

**3** One person keeps an old diary written during World War II by his
or her Aunt Maud.

**4** Whatever Angela keeps in her safety deposit box wasn't
formerly owned by a female relative.

**5** Bill has an antique silver teapot in his safety deposit box.

|  | Brooch | Diary | Painting | Teapot | Watch | Aunt Maud | Father | Grandmother | Mother | Uncle Pete |
|---|---|---|---|---|---|---|---|---|---|---|
| Angela |  |  |  |  |  |  |  |  |  |  |
| Bill |  |  |  |  |  |  |  |  |  |  |
| Claire |  |  |  |  |  |  |  |  |  |  |
| Judy |  |  |  |  |  |  |  |  |  |  |
| Mike |  |  |  |  |  |  |  |  |  |  |
| Aunt Maud |  |  |  |  |  |
| Father |  |  |  |  |  |
| Grandmother |  |  |  |  |  |
| Mother |  |  |  |  |  |
| Uncle Pete |  |  |  |  |  |

| Customer | Item | Relative |
|---|---|---|
|  |  |  |
|  |  |  |
|  |  |  |
|  |  |  |
|  |  |  |

# Mugs Shot

Use the clues to identify the owner of each mug in the line-up below, together with its shade and current contents.

1 The mug of warm milk is immediately next to and between the red mug and the one belonging to Richard.
2 The mug of tea is immediately next to and right of the white mug.
3 Harriet's green mug contains water and is further left than Len's mug.
4 Len's mug is further right than Margaret's.
5 Margaret's mug doesn't contain coffee.

|  | Harriet | Len | Margaret | Richard | Green | Red | White | Yellow | Coffee | Milk | Tea | Water |
|---|---|---|---|---|---|---|---|---|---|---|---|---|
| Mug A |  |  |  |  |  |  |  |  |  |  |  |  |
| Mug B |  |  |  |  |  |  |  |  |  |  |  |  |
| Mug C |  |  |  |  |  |  |  |  |  |  |  |  |
| Mug D |  |  |  |  |  |  |  |  |  |  |  |  |
| Coffee |  |  |  |  |  |  |  |  |  |  |  |  |
| Milk |  |  |  |  |  |  |  |  |  |  |  |  |
| Tea |  |  |  |  |  |  |  |  |  |  |  |  |
| Water |  |  |  |  |  |  |  |  |  |  |  |  |
| Green |  |  |  |  |  |  |  |  |  |  |  |  |
| Red |  |  |  |  |  |  |  |  |  |  |  |  |
| White |  |  |  |  |  |  |  |  |  |  |  |  |
| Yellow |  |  |  |  |  |  |  |  |  |  |  |  |

LEFT ⇐   RIGHT ⇒

A B C D

| Mug | Owner | Shade | Contents |
|---|---|---|---|
|  |  |  |  |
|  |  |  |  |
|  |  |  |  |
|  |  |  |  |

# Chest Problem

The local auctioneers are having a sale of pre-World War I furniture. Included in their brochure are the four chests you see in the diagram below. Can you correctly identify each in terms of the wood in which it is made, the name of its maker, and the year it was produced?

1. Item A was either made by Wood & Co or it's the oak chest, which was produced four years earlier than that made by Wood & Co.

2. The cedar chest (not item B) is pictured next to the one built in 1900.

3. The chest produced in 1914 is further right than the one made by Forresters, which was produced four years after the walnut chest.

4. The chest made of oak was made either ten years earlier or ten years later than the one shown as D in the diagram below.

5. The chest made in 1914 is next to two others: the pine chest (not item D) and that made by L Turner.

|  | Wood | | | | Maker | | | | Year | | | |
|---|---|---|---|---|---|---|---|---|---|---|---|---|
|  | Cedar | Oak | Pine | Walnut | Axe Bros | Forresters | L Turner | Wood & Co | 1900 | 1904 | 1910 | 1914 |
| Chest A |  |  |  |  |  |  |  |  |  |  |  |  |
| Chest B |  |  |  |  |  |  |  |  |  |  |  |  |
| Chest C |  |  |  |  |  |  |  |  |  |  |  |  |
| Chest D |  |  |  |  |  |  |  |  |  |  |  |  |
| 1900 |  |  |  |  |  |  |  |  |  |  |  |  |
| 1904 |  |  |  |  |  |  |  |  |  |  |  |  |
| 1910 |  |  |  |  |  |  |  |  |  |  |  |  |
| 1914 |  |  |  |  |  |  |  |  |  |  |  |  |
| Axe Bros |  |  |  |  |  |  |  |  |  |  |  |  |
| Forresters |  |  |  |  |  |  |  |  |  |  |  |  |
| L Turner |  |  |  |  |  |  |  |  |  |  |  |  |
| Wood & Co |  |  |  |  |  |  |  |  |  |  |  |  |

LEFT ⇦    RIGHT ⇨

A  B  C  D

| Chest | Wood | Maker | Year |
|---|---|---|---|
|  |  |  |  |
|  |  |  |  |
|  |  |  |  |
|  |  |  |  |

# Three-Legged Racers

In a three-legged race, contestants run in pairs: the right leg of one partner is joined to the left leg of the other. The pair then link arms and try to run by moving the tied legs first, then (at the same time as each other) they move their "free" legs. Can you discover who partnered whom in the race in which these people participated, as well as their finishing position?

1   Bob partnered Danny. They weren't the last of the five pairs to cross the finishing line, nor were they the third pair to finish the race.

2   Colin and his partner finished the race ahead of everyone else.

3   Ian and his partner were second in the race.

4   Eddie and his partner finished ten yards ahead of Geoff and his partner.

5   Joe and his partner finished ahead of Adam and his partner (who wasn't Martin).

|  | Partner 2 | | | | | Position | | | | |
| --- | --- | --- | --- | --- | --- | --- | --- | --- | --- | --- |
|  | Adam | Danny | Geoff | Henry | Ian | First | Second | Third | Fourth | Fifth |
| Bob |  |  |  |  |  |  |  |  |  |  |
| Colin |  |  |  |  |  |  |  |  |  |  |
| Eddie |  |  |  |  |  |  |  |  |  |  |
| Joe |  |  |  |  |  |  |  |  |  |  |
| Martin |  |  |  |  |  |  |  |  |  |  |
| First |  |  |  |  |  |  |  |  |  |  |
| Second |  |  |  |  |  |  |  |  |  |  |
| Third |  |  |  |  |  |  |  |  |  |  |
| Fourth |  |  |  |  |  |  |  |  |  |  |
| Fifth |  |  |  |  |  |  |  |  |  |  |

| Partner 1 | Partner 2 | Position |
| --- | --- | --- |
|  |  |  |
|  |  |  |
|  |  |  |
|  |  |  |
|  |  |  |

# Slimming Down

Five friends have been attending weight-loss clinics over the past eighteen months, meeting with various degrees of success in their efforts to lose weight. What were their weights at the start of the sessions, and what are their weights today?

1  All five women have lost weight since starting the classes.

2  Lolita (Lolly to her friends, including you!) was heavier than Holly at the start of the weight-loss clinics.

3  Dolly has lost a total of twenty pounds. She is currently heavier than Polly, whereas at the start of the sessions, Polly was heavier than Dolly.

4  The woman who used to weigh 215 pounds now weighs 208 pounds.

5  Molly (who isn't the heaviest of the five women today) isn't exactly three pounds heavier than Polly.

6  Only one woman has lost exactly ten pounds.

|  | Start | | | | | Today | | | | |
|---|---|---|---|---|---|---|---|---|---|---|
|  | 210 lbs | 215 lbs | 220 lbs | 225 lbs | 230 lbs | 200 lbs | 203 lbs | 205 lbs | 208 lbs | 210 lbs |
| Dolly |  |  |  |  |  |  |  |  |  |  |
| Holly |  |  |  |  |  |  |  |  |  |  |
| Lolly |  |  |  |  |  |  |  |  |  |  |
| Molly |  |  |  |  |  |  |  |  |  |  |
| Polly |  |  |  |  |  |  |  |  |  |  |
| 200 lbs |  |  |  |  |  |  |  |  |  |  |
| 203 lbs |  |  |  |  |  |  |  |  |  |  |
| 205 lbs |  |  |  |  |  |  |  |  |  |  |
| 208 lbs |  |  |  |  |  |  |  |  |  |  |
| 210 lbs |  |  |  |  |  |  |  |  |  |  |

Today

| Slimmer | Start | Today |
|---|---|---|
|  |  |  |
|  |  |  |
|  |  |  |
|  |  |  |
|  |  |  |

# Birthday Presents

Anne's four nieces all celebrate birthdays on different days
next week. Use the clues below to discover which present each
girl will receive from Anne, together with the day of the week
on which each one's birthday falls, and her current age.

1 Joanne's birthday is the day before that of the girl who will get
a poster of her pop star idol, but the day after that of the eight-
year-old.

2 The girl who will receive a book from her Aunt Anne is two years
older than the one who celebrates her birthday on Wednesday.

3 The seven-year-old will be receiving a pair of slippers from her
Aunt Anne. Her birthday is earlier in the week than that of the
oldest girl, but later in the week than Polly's birthday.

4 Mary isn't the youngest of Anne's four nieces.

|  | Gift | | | | Day | | | | Age | | | |
|---|---|---|---|---|---|---|---|---|---|---|---|---|
|  | Book | Poster | Slippers | Video | Tuesday | Wednesday | Thursday | Friday | 6 | 7 | 8 | 9 |
| Joanne |  |  |  |  |  |  |  |  |  |  |  |  |
| Mary |  |  |  |  |  |  |  |  |  |  |  |  |
| Polly |  |  |  |  |  |  |  |  |  |  |  |  |
| Susan |  |  |  |  |  |  |  |  |  |  |  |  |
| 6 years old |  |  |  |  |  |  |  |  |  |  |  |  |
| 7 years old |  |  |  |  |  |  |  |  |  |  |  |  |
| 8 years old |  |  |  |  |  |  |  |  |  |  |  |  |
| 9 years old |  |  |  |  |  |  |  |  |  |  |  |  |
| Tuesday |  |  |  |  |  |  |  |  |  |  |  |  |
| Wednesday |  |  |  |  |  |  |  |  |  |  |  |  |
| Thursday |  |  |  |  |  |  |  |  |  |  |  |  |
| Friday |  |  |  |  |  |  |  |  |  |  |  |  |

| Niece | Gift | Day | Age |
|---|---|---|---|
|  |  |  |  |
|  |  |  |  |
|  |  |  |  |
|  |  |  |  |

# The Four Seasons

Four works of art are currently on display in the foyer of the Berthold Institute. Can you discover which artist (first name and last name) painted each, and the year in which each was produced?

1 *Spring* was completed three years earlier than the painting by Max Dawkins.

2 The artist named Fischer completed his or her picture in an earlier year than that painted by Pearl.

3 *Summer* is the work of Xandra, whose last name isn't Fischer or Maine.

4 Roy produced the work entitled *Winter*.

|  | Artist | | | | Last name | | | | Year | | | |
|---|---|---|---|---|---|---|---|---|---|---|---|---|
|  | Max | Pearl | Roy | Xandra | Clark | Dawkins | Fischer | Maine | 2002 | 2003 | 2005 | 2006 |
| Spring |  |  |  |  |  |  |  |  |  |  |  |  |
| Summer |  |  |  |  |  |  |  |  |  |  |  |  |
| Autumn |  |  |  |  |  |  |  |  |  |  |  |  |
| Winter |  |  |  |  |  |  |  |  |  |  |  |  |
| 2002 |  |  |  |  |  |  |  |  |  |  |  |  |
| 2003 |  |  |  |  |  |  |  |  |  |  |  |  |
| 2005 |  |  |  |  |  |  |  |  |  |  |  |  |
| 2006 |  |  |  |  |  |  |  |  |  |  |  |  |
| Clark |  |  |  |  |  |  |  |  |  |  |  |  |
| Dawkins |  |  |  |  |  |  |  |  |  |  |  |  |
| Fischer |  |  |  |  |  |  |  |  |  |  |  |  |
| Maine |  |  |  |  |  |  |  |  |  |  |  |  |

| Work | Artist | Last name | Year |
|---|---|---|---|
|  |  |  |  |
|  |  |  |  |
|  |  |  |  |
|  |  |  |  |

# Free Samples

It's amazing how many free samples of various new products were sent to five friends last week. Can you work through the clues to discover how many domestic (for household use) and personal (for use on the body) samples everyone received?

1. No-one received precisely the same number of domestic free samples as personal free samples.
2. The man who received eight sachets of hair shampoo (for personal use) also received three sachets of carpet shampoo (for domestic use).
3. Alan received three fewer free samples of personal products than the quantity of free samples of domestic products received by Bertie.
4. Jenny received two more free samples of personal products than the number of free samples of domestic products received by Kate.
5. Micky didn't receive exactly one fewer domestic free sample than Kate.

|  | Domestic | | | | | Personal | | | | |
|---|---|---|---|---|---|---|---|---|---|---|
|  | 3 | 4 | 5 | 6 | 7 | 4 | 5 | 6 | 7 | 8 |
| Alan |  |  |  |  |  |  |  |  |  |  |
| Bertie |  |  |  |  |  |  |  |  |  |  |
| Jenny |  |  |  |  |  |  |  |  |  |  |
| Kate |  |  |  |  |  |  |  |  |  |  |
| Micky |  |  |  |  |  |  |  |  |  |  |
| 4 |  |  |  |  |  |
| 5 |  |  |  |  |  |
| 6 |  |  |  |  |  |
| 7 |  |  |  |  |  |
| 8 |  |  |  |  |  |

(Left axis label: Personal)

| Friend | Domestic | Personal |
|---|---|---|
|  |  |  |
|  |  |  |
|  |  |  |
|  |  |  |
|  |  |  |

# Radio Ga Ga

**18**

On five separate occasions last week, DJ Ivor Smallbrane played *Radio Ga Ga* by Queen, then attributed the recording to another group, thus incurring the wrath of his producer, as well as receiving a number of complaints from listeners. Can you work out on which day he attributed *Radio Ga Ga* to each of the listed groups, as well as the number of telephone calls of complaint received by the studio that day?

1　There were thirteen fewer calls of complaint made to the studios on Tuesday than the number received when Ivor attributed *Radio Ga Ga* to Abba.

2　The Beach Boys were credited with the song two days before it was attributed to ZZ Top, but later in the week than the day on which the lowest number of calls was received.

3　The Beatles being mentioned in connection with the song drew eight more complaints than were received on Thursday.

4　DJ Ivor Smallbrane made no mention of the Rolling Stones on Monday.

5　More calls of complaint were received on Wednesday than on Friday.

|  | Group | | | | | Complaints | | | | |
|---|---|---|---|---|---|---|---|---|---|---|
|  | Abba | Beach Boys | Beatles | Rolling Stones | ZZ Top | 29 | 37 | 42 | 50 | 55 |
| Monday |  |  |  |  |  |  |  |  |  |  |
| Tuesday |  |  |  |  |  |  |  |  |  |  |
| Wednesday |  |  |  |  |  |  |  |  |  |  |
| Thursday |  |  |  |  |  |  |  |  |  |  |
| Friday |  |  |  |  |  |  |  |  |  |  |
| 29 complaints |  |  |  |  |  |  |  |  |  |  |
| 37 complaints |  |  |  |  |  |  |  |  |  |  |
| 42 complaints |  |  |  |  |  |  |  |  |  |  |
| 50 complaints |  |  |  |  |  |  |  |  |  |  |
| 55 complaints |  |  |  |  |  |  |  |  |  |  |

| Day | Group | Complaints |
|---|---|---|
|  |  |  |
|  |  |  |
|  |  |  |
|  |  |  |
|  |  |  |

# Unhappy New Year!

Four women sent just one New Year card last year and (embarrassingly) received just one, from one of the other three – to whom her own card had not been addressed! What is each woman's full name, to whom did she send a card, and on which date was it posted?

1 Alice posted a card to Tammy (whose last name isn't Davis) on 28 December.

2 Vera (who didn't post a card on 29 December) sent one to Naomi Jones.

3 Naomi posted a card on 30 December.

4 Tammy didn't send a card to the woman named Wright, nor is Tammy's last name Wright.

|  | Last name | | | | Sent to | | | | 27 December | 28 December | 29 December | 30 December |
|---|---|---|---|---|---|---|---|---|---|---|---|---|
|  | Davis | Jones | Morgan | Wright | Alice | Naomi | Tammy | Vera | | | | |
| Alice |  |  |  |  |  |  |  |  |  |  |  |  |
| Naomi |  |  |  |  |  |  |  |  |  |  |  |  |
| Tammy |  |  |  |  |  |  |  |  |  |  |  |  |
| Vera |  |  |  |  |  |  |  |  |  |  |  |  |
| 27 December |  |  |  |  |  |  |  |  | | | | |
| 28 December |  |  |  |  |  |  |  |  | | | | |
| 29 December |  |  |  |  |  |  |  |  | | | | |
| 30 December |  |  |  |  |  |  |  |  | | | | |
| Sent to Alice |  |  |  |  | | | | | | | | |
| Sent to Naomi |  |  |  |  | | | | | | | | |
| Sent to Tammy |  |  |  |  | | | | | | | | |
| Sent to Vera |  |  |  |  | | | | | | | | |

| Name | Last name | Sent to | Date |
|---|---|---|---|
|  |  |  |  |
|  |  |  |  |
|  |  |  |  |
|  |  |  |  |

# 20

# January Sales

The couples in this puzzle spent rather more than they intended in this year's January sales, even though the goods they bought had been greatly reduced from their original prices. Find out who is married to whom, what they bought, and how much they spent.

1 The couple who bought the washing machine spent more than David and his wife, but less than Theresa and her husband.

2 Brian and his wife spent $40 less than Katy and her husband.

3 The computer cost $20 less than the dishwasher.

4 Brian's wife's name has the same number of letters as that of Paul's wife.

|  | Wife | | | | Bought | | | | Spent | | | |
|---|---|---|---|---|---|---|---|---|---|---|---|---|
|  | Annie | Katy | Theresa | Zara | Computer | Dishwasher | DVD player | W. machine | $150 | $170 | $190 | $230 |
| Brian |  |  |  |  |  |  |  |  |  |  |  |  |
| David |  |  |  |  |  |  |  |  |  |  |  |  |
| Paul |  |  |  |  |  |  |  |  |  |  |  |  |
| William |  |  |  |  |  |  |  |  |  |  |  |  |
| $150 |  |  |  |  |  |  |  |  |  |  |  |  |
| $170 |  |  |  |  |  |  |  |  |  |  |  |  |
| $190 |  |  |  |  |  |  |  |  |  |  |  |  |
| $230 |  |  |  |  |  |  |  |  |  |  |  |  |
| Computer |  |  |  |  |  |  |  |  |  |  |  |  |
| Dishwasher |  |  |  |  |  |  |  |  |  |  |  |  |
| DVD player |  |  |  |  |  |  |  |  |  |  |  |  |
| W. machine |  |  |  |  |  |  |  |  |  |  |  |  |

| Husband | Wife | Bought | Spent |
|---|---|---|---|
|  |  |  |  |
|  |  |  |  |
|  |  |  |  |
|  |  |  |  |

# Soup Story

21

Five students each took soup for their lunch at school today.
How old is each, and what soup was in his or her thermos?

**1** Dean is one year older than the student whose thermos contained tomato soup, but one year younger than the student who took a thermos of potato soup to school today.

**2** Jeremy is one year older than Nicole, whose thermos contained chicken soup.

**3** The student whose thermos contained beef soup is two years older than Robert.

**4** Elaine is younger than at least one of the other students, perhaps more!

|  | Age | | | | | Soup | | | | |
|---|---|---|---|---|---|---|---|---|---|---|
|  | 13 | 14 | 15 | 16 | 17 | Beef | Chicken | Onion | Potato | Tomato |
| Dean |  |  |  |  |  |  |  |  |  |  |
| Elaine |  |  |  |  |  |  |  |  |  |  |
| Jeremy |  |  |  |  |  |  |  |  |  |  |
| Nicole |  |  |  |  |  |  |  |  |  |  |
| Robert |  |  |  |  |  |  |  |  |  |  |
| Beef |  |  |  |  |  |
| Chicken |  |  |  |  |  |
| Onion |  |  |  |  |  |
| Potato |  |  |  |  |  |
| Tomato |  |  |  |  |  |

| Student | Age | Soup |
|---|---|---|
|  |  |  |
|  |  |  |
|  |  |  |
|  |  |  |
|  |  |  |

**22**

# The Maze

Five friends recently visited a maze (rather a challenging one, with very high hedges) and, after eventually locating the middle, decided to hold a contest to see who could get out the quickest! Each took a different route out, but how long will it take you to get through this puzzle? You need to find out the number of the route each chose, and the length of time he or she took to get out.

1 The route taken by Abigail is numbered two higher than the route taken by the man who took two minutes longer than Simon to exit the maze.

2 The route taken by the person who got out after 17 minutes is numbered one higher than that taken by Emma, but one lower than that taken by Greg.

3 Simon chose a route with a higher number than that taken by the person who got out in 15 minutes, but a lower number than that chosen by Theodore.

4 The person who chose route 4 didn't take exactly 16 minutes to leave the maze.

| | Route | | | | | Time (minutes) | | | | |
|---|---|---|---|---|---|---|---|---|---|---|
| | 1 | 2 | 3 | 4 | 5 | 15 | 16 | 17 | 18 | 19 |
| Abigail | | | | | | | | | | |
| Emma | | | | | | | | | | |
| Greg | | | | | | | | | | |
| Simon | | | | | | | | | | |
| Theodore | | | | | | | | | | |
| 15 minutes | | | | | | | | | | |
| 16 minutes | | | | | | | | | | |
| 17 minutes | | | | | | | | | | |
| 18 minutes | | | | | | | | | | |
| 19 minutes | | | | | | | | | | |

| Friend | Route | Time |
|---|---|---|
| | | |
| | | |
| | | |
| | | |
| | | |

# Model Children

Four teachers at the local school decided to hold a model-making day and asked their pupils to bring in cardboard boxes and tubes, which could be used. Discover the full name of each teacher, and the two different quantities of boxes and tubes collected by their pupils.

1  The pupils of the teacher named Harper brought in the same quantity of boxes as the number of tubes brought in by Rosa's pupils.

2  Miss Palmer's pupils brought in the highest number of boxes and the lowest number of tubes.

3  The total quantity of boxes and tubes brought in by Louise's pupils was exactly the same as the total quantity of boxes and tubes brought in by the pupils of the teacher named Davis.

4  Joseph's pupils brought in more boxes than Jim's pupils. Jim's pupils didn't bring the greatest quantity of tubes.

|  | Last name | | | | Boxes | | | | Tubes | | | |
|---|---|---|---|---|---|---|---|---|---|---|---|---|
|  | Davis | Harper | Mitchell | Palmer | 21 | 24 | 26 | 29 | 14 | 17 | 21 | 24 |
| Jim |  |  |  |  |  |  |  |  |  |  |  |  |
| Louise |  |  |  |  |  |  |  |  |  |  |  |  |
| Joseph |  |  |  |  |  |  |  |  |  |  |  |  |
| Rosa |  |  |  |  |  |  |  |  |  |  |  |  |
| 14 tubes |  |  |  |  |  |  |  |  |
| 17 tubes |  |  |  |  |  |  |  |  |
| 21 tubes |  |  |  |  |  |  |  |  |
| 24 tubes |  |  |  |  |  |  |  |  |
| 21 boxes |  |  |  |  |
| 24 boxes |  |  |  |  |
| 26 boxes |  |  |  |  |
| 29 boxes |  |  |  |  |

| Teacher | Last name | Boxes | Tubes |
|---|---|---|---|
|  |  |  |  |
|  |  |  |  |
|  |  |  |  |
|  |  |  |  |

# New Employment

Four men who have been unemployed are due to start work next week for new companies. Discover each man's occupation, the day of the week on which he will start his new job, and the length of time for which he had been out of work.

1  Fred is an accountant and will start his new job the day after Geoff, who had been unemployed for two weeks longer than Fred.

2  The driver (not Randy) will start his new job the day after the man who works as a furniture salesman.

3  The car mechanic is due to start later in the week than Randy.

4  The man who had been out of work for ten weeks starts his new job on Thursday of next week.

|  | Position | | | | Starts | | | | Unemployed | | | |
|---|---|---|---|---|---|---|---|---|---|---|---|---|
|  | Accountant | Car mechanic | Driver | Salesman | Monday | Tuesday | Wednesday | Thursday | 8 weeks | 9 weeks | 10 weeks | 11 weeks |
| Dan |  |  |  |  |  |  |  |  |  |  |  |  |
| Fred |  |  |  |  |  |  |  |  |  |  |  |  |
| Geoff |  |  |  |  |  |  |  |  |  |  |  |  |
| Randy |  |  |  |  |  |  |  |  |  |  |  |  |
| 8 weeks |  |  |  |  |  |  |  |  |
| 9 weeks |  |  |  |  |  |  |  |  |
| 10 weeks |  |  |  |  |  |  |  |  |
| 11 weeks |  |  |  |  |  |  |  |  |
| Monday |  |  |  |  |
| Tuesday |  |  |  |  |
| Wednesday |  |  |  |  |
| Thursday |  |  |  |  |

| Name | Position | Starts | Weeks |
|---|---|---|---|
|  |  |  |  |
|  |  |  |  |
|  |  |  |  |
|  |  |  |  |

# Pieces of Pizza

The pizza you see below is topped with green olives and black olives (the green ones are shown as white in the picture). Every one of the people listed in the grid will get a slice. Can you discover their full names, and say which piece each will receive?

**1** Mrs Butcher's slice has the same number of black olives as the piece that Della Morgan will receive.

**2** Mr Sullivan's piece has the same number of green olives as the slice that will be given to Candice (whose last name isn't Knowles).

**3** Neither Candice nor Della will receive a slice of pizza with a total of five olives on the top.

**4** The slice destined for Beryl's plate has a total of one more olive than Alan's piece of pizza.

| | Last name | | | | | Piece | | | | |
|---|---|---|---|---|---|---|---|---|---|---|
| | Butcher | Knowles | Morgan | Rousseau | Sullivan | 1 | 2 | 3 | 4 | 5 |
| Alan | | | | | | | | | | |
| Beryl | | | | | | | | | | |
| Candice | | | | | | | | | | |
| Della | | | | | | | | | | |
| Edward | | | | | | | | | | |
| Piece 1 | | | | | | | | | | |
| Piece 2 | | | | | | | | | | |
| Piece 3 | | | | | | | | | | |
| Piece 4 | | | | | | | | | | |
| Piece 5 | | | | | | | | | | |

| Name | Last name | Piece |
|---|---|---|
| | | |
| | | |
| | | |
| | | |
| | | |

# Birthdays

Five couples celebrated birthdays on various days (Monday to Sunday) of last week, and no man's birthday fell on the same day as that of his wife. Use the clues to discover the birthdays of the two people in each case.

1 Bill's birthday was two days later than that of the woman married to the man who celebrated his birthday on Tuesday.

2 Mike's birthday was the day after that of his wife.

3 Nancy's birthday was the day after that of Kay's husband.

|  | His birthday | | | | | Her birthday | | | | |
|---|---|---|---|---|---|---|---|---|---|---|
|  | Monday | Tuesday | Thursday | Friday | Saturday | Monday | Tuesday | Wednesday | Friday | Sunday |
| Bill and Joy |  |  |  |  |  |  |  |  |  |  |
| David and Kay |  |  |  |  |  |  |  |  |  |  |
| Mike and Louise |  |  |  |  |  |  |  |  |  |  |
| Pete and Nancy |  |  |  |  |  |  |  |  |  |  |
| Roger and Lynne |  |  |  |  |  |  |  |  |  |  |
| Her birthday — Monday |  |  |  |  |  |  |
| Her birthday — Tuesday |  |  |  |  |  |  |
| Her birthday — Wednesday |  |  |  |  |  |  |
| Her birthday — Friday |  |  |  |  |  |  |
| Her birthday — Sunday |  |  |  |  |  |  |

| Couple | His | Hers |
|---|---|---|
|  |  |  |
|  |  |  |
|  |  |  |
|  |  |  |
|  |  |  |

# End of Semester

Mr & Mrs Barton have four children at different schools, all due to close for the holidays on different days next week. Can you match each child to his or her age, the name of the school he or she attends, and the last day of the semester at each?

1  The last day at St John's is the day before that at Bayside which, in turn, is the day before that of the school attended by Tammy.

2  The child (not Paul) who attends St John's school is younger than the child whose last day of the semester is Wednesday of next week.

3  Tammy is three years older than Martin. The last day at Martin's school is the day after that at Applewood.

4  Cathy isn't the youngest child in the Barton family.

|  | Age | | | | School | | | | Last day | | | |
|---|---|---|---|---|---|---|---|---|---|---|---|---|
|  | 6 | 7 | 9 | 10 | Applewood | Bayside | Mount View | St John's | Tuesday | Wednesday | Thursday | Friday |
| Cathy |  |  |  |  |  |  |  |  |  |  |  |  |
| Martin |  |  |  |  |  |  |  |  |  |  |  |  |
| Paul |  |  |  |  |  |  |  |  |  |  |  |  |
| Tammy |  |  |  |  |  |  |  |  |  |  |  |  |
| Tuesday |  |  |  |  |  |  |  |  |
| Wednesday |  |  |  |  |  |  |  |  |
| Thursday |  |  |  |  |  |  |  |  |
| Friday |  |  |  |  |  |  |  |  |
| Applewood |  |  |  |  |
| Bayside |  |  |  |  |
| Mount View |  |  |  |  |
| St John's |  |  |  |  |

| Child | Age | School | Last day |
|---|---|---|---|
|  |  |  |  |
|  |  |  |  |
|  |  |  |  |
|  |  |  |  |

# Pie-eating Contest

Four men who entered a pie-eating contest made it through to the finale, held exactly one month after the trials (to give their stomachs a break!). On the day, each adopted a nickname, and chose a fruit filling for his pies. What was each man's nickname, what did he choose to eat, and how many did he manage to consume in the allotted time?

1 The man nicknamed "Buster" chose the pies filled with apple. He managed to eat two more than Gus, but fewer than the man who had chosen the cherry pies.

2 "Hungry" Hal ate more pies than Dave, but fewer than the quantity of peach pies which one of the men managed to consume.

3 The man who chose a filling of rhubarb isn't nicknamed "Ravenous".

|  | Nickname | | | | Filling | | | | Quantity | | | |
|---|---|---|---|---|---|---|---|---|---|---|---|---|
|  | Buster | Greedy | Hungry | Ravenous | Apple | Cherry | Peach | Rhubarb | 18 | 20 | 22 | 24 |
| Dave |  |  |  |  |  |  |  |  |  |  |  |  |
| Ferdy |  |  |  |  |  |  |  |  |  |  |  |  |
| Gus |  |  |  |  |  |  |  |  |  |  |  |  |
| Hal |  |  |  |  |  |  |  |  |  |  |  |  |
| 18 pies |  |  |  |  |  |  |  |  |
| 20 pies |  |  |  |  |  |  |  |  |
| 22 pies |  |  |  |  |  |  |  |  |
| 24 pies |  |  |  |  |  |  |  |  |
| Apple |  |  |  |  |
| Cherry |  |  |  |  |
| Peach |  |  |  |  |
| Rhubarb |  |  |  |  |

| Name | Nickname | Filling | Quantity |
|---|---|---|---|
|  |  |  |  |
|  |  |  |  |
|  |  |  |  |
|  |  |  |  |

# Hair Appointments

The five women who live in the houses shown on the plan below are currently at the hairdresser's salon, having their hair styled. Can you discover where each woman lives, and the details of her hair?

1   The woman with blond hair lives next to and south of Adele, who lives directly east of Laura.

2   Sarah lives next to and south of Molly.

3   One of the five women lives directly east of Jane, who lives further north than the woman with silver hair.

4   The woman with chestnut hair lives next to and north of the woman with black hair.

| | House No | | | | | Hair | | | | |
|---|---|---|---|---|---|---|---|---|---|---|
| | 1 | 2 | 3 | 4 | 5 | Black | Blond | Brown | Chestnut | Silver |
| Adele | | | | | | | | | | |
| Jane | | | | | | | | | | |
| Laura | | | | | | | | | | |
| Molly | | | | | | | | | | |
| Sarah | | | | | | | | | | |
| Black | | | | | | | | | | |
| Blond | | | | | | | | | | |
| Brown | | | | | | | | | | |
| Chestnut | | | | | | | | | | |
| Silver | | | | | | | | | | |

N
W — E
S

| 1 | | 2 |
|---|---|---|
| 3 | | 4 |
| | | 5 |

| Name | House No | Hair |
|---|---|---|
| | | |
| | | |
| | | |
| | | |
| | | |

**30**

# Tooth Trouble

In January and February of this year, each of these five people found it necessary to make two trips to the dentist, once in January and once in February (the latter being for an extraction of the troublesome tooth). Can you discover the date of each person's first and second appointments?

1 Alicia's first appointment was on the same date in January as the date of Fred's February appointment, which was earlier in the month than Colette's February appointment.

2 Bernard's first appointment was later than Colette's, but earlier than Tracey's first appointment (which wasn't on 31 January).

3 Whoever saw the dentist on 11 January had a tooth extracted five days before Tracey's second appointment. Tracey's second appointment was earlier than Bernard's second appointment.

4 Alicia's second appointment wasn't on 19 February.

|  | First | | | | | Second | | | | |
|---|---|---|---|---|---|---|---|---|---|---|
|  | 5 January | 11 January | 17 January | 24 January | 31 January | 5 February | 10 February | 15 February | 17 February | 19 February |
| Alicia |  |  |  |  |  |  |  |  |  |  |
| Bernard |  |  |  |  |  |  |  |  |  |  |
| Colette |  |  |  |  |  |  |  |  |  |  |
| Fred |  |  |  |  |  |  |  |  |  |  |
| Tracey |  |  |  |  |  |  |  |  |  |  |
| 5 February |  |  |  |  |  |
| 10 February |  |  |  |  |  |
| 15 February |  |  |  |  |  |
| 17 February |  |  |  |  |  |
| 19 February |  |  |  |  |  |

| Name | January | February |
|---|---|---|
|  |  |  |
|  |  |  |
|  |  |  |
|  |  |  |
|  |  |  |

# Zodiac

The twelve people in this puzzle were born under different star signs, and of the twelve, there are four husbands, four wives and four daughters, one of each in the same family, and sharing the same last name. Can you match the three family members and their respective star signs?

1  The Gemini daughter was born to the Cancerian and his wife, whose star sign isn't Scorpio. The woman born in Scorpio isn't Mrs Carter.

2  Miss Carter was born under the sign of Leo.

3  Neither the Piscean nor the man whose star sign is Aries is married to the Libran.

4  The woman born under the sign of Libra has a Sagittarian daughter, unlike Mrs Adamson.

5  Mr Brent was born in the sign of Aries.

6  The woman born under the sign of Aquarius isn't married to the Piscean.

|  | Husband | | | | Wife | | | | Daughter | | | |
|---|---|---|---|---|---|---|---|---|---|---|---|---|
|  | Aries | Cancer | Virgo | Pisces | Taurus | Libra | Scorpio | Aquarius | Gemini | Leo | Sagittarius | Capricorn |
| Adamson |  |  |  |  |  |  |  |  |  |  |  |  |
| Brent |  |  |  |  |  |  |  |  |  |  |  |  |
| Carter |  |  |  |  |  |  |  |  |  |  |  |  |
| Dale |  |  |  |  |  |  |  |  |  |  |  |  |
| Gemini (Daughter) |  |  |  |  |  |  |  |  |  |  |  |  |
| Leo (Daughter) |  |  |  |  |  |  |  |  |  |  |  |  |
| Sagittarius (Daughter) |  |  |  |  |  |  |  |  |  |  |  |  |
| Capricorn (Daughter) |  |  |  |  |  |  |  |  |  |  |  |  |
| Taurus (Wife) |  |  |  |  |  |  |  |  |  |  |  |  |
| Libra (Wife) |  |  |  |  |  |  |  |  |  |  |  |  |
| Scorpio (Wife) |  |  |  |  |  |  |  |  |  |  |  |  |
| Aquarius (Wife) |  |  |  |  |  |  |  |  |  |  |  |  |

| Last name | Husband | Wife | Daughter |
|---|---|---|---|
|  |  |  |  |
|  |  |  |  |
|  |  |  |  |
|  |  |  |  |

# Community Events

The community hall is booked by local clubs for the first four nights of each week. Every club is run by a different person, and starts at a different time. Can you discover which club each person organizes, and the evening and time it takes place?

1 The club held on Monday evenings starts half an hour later than the drama club, which is held earlier in the week than Thursday. Miss Payne doesn't organize the drama club.

2 Mr Willard's book club meets the evening before the club run by Mr Jackson, which starts fifteen minutes later than the walking club.

3 The walking club meets earlier in the week than the club which starts at eight o'clock.

|  | Book | Camera | Drama | Walking | Monday | Tuesday | Wednesday | Thursday | 7.00pm | 7.30pm | 7.45pm | 8.00pm |
|---|---|---|---|---|---|---|---|---|---|---|---|---|
| Mrs Hunter | | | | | | | | | | | | |
| Mr Jackson | | | | | | | | | | | | |
| Miss Payne | | | | | | | | | | | | |
| Mr Willard | | | | | | | | | | | | |
| 7.00pm | | | | | | | | | | | | |
| 7.30pm | | | | | | | | | | | | |
| 7.45pm | | | | | | | | | | | | |
| 8.00pm | | | | | | | | | | | | |
| Monday | | | | | | | | | | | | |
| Tuesday | | | | | | | | | | | | |
| Wednesday | | | | | | | | | | | | |
| Thursday | | | | | | | | | | | | |

| Name | Club | Evening | Time |
|---|---|---|---|
| | | | |
| | | | |
| | | | |
| | | | |

# Carol's Cards

Carol sent five cards on different dates last month. What type of card did each person receive, and on which date did Carol post it?

1 The card to Adrian was posted earlier than the one congratulating someone on a new job, but later than the card addressed to Beatrice.

2 Raymond received a card from Carol on the day that he moved into his new home; and Raymond's new home card was posted two days later than the one congratulating one of the two women on the birth of a daughter.

3 Carol posted a birthday card on the 15th.

| | Type | | | | | Posted | | | | |
|---|---|---|---|---|---|---|---|---|---|---|
| | Birthday | Get well | New baby | New home | New job | 11th | 15th | 17th | 20th | 22nd |
| Adrian | | | | | | | | | | |
| Beatrice | | | | | | | | | | |
| Raymond | | | | | | | | | | |
| Sheila | | | | | | | | | | |
| Terence | | | | | | | | | | |
| 11th | | | | | | | | | | |
| 15th | | | | | | | | | | |
| 17th | | | | | | | | | | |
| 20th | | | | | | | | | | |
| 22nd | | | | | | | | | | |

| Recipient | Type | Posted |
|---|---|---|
| | | |
| | | |
| | | |
| | | |
| | | |

# After School

Prince Rupert School offers two clubs after school. Every evening a different activity can be enjoyed in the Sports Club, and a different subject can be more closely taught in the Study Club. How many pupils attended the clubs on each evening of last week?

1 The number of pupils who attended Wednesday's Study Club was three lower than the number of pupils at Friday's Sports Club.

2 On one of the evenings, 17 pupils attended the Sports Club and 22 pupils attended the Study Club. This was not the evening before 19 attended the Study Club.

3 There were three more pupils at the Sports Club than at the Study Club on Tuesday.

4 There were three more pupils at Thursday's Sports Club than had attended Monday's Sports Club; and more at Monday's Sports Club than at Monday's Study Club.

|  | Sports | | | | | Study | | | | |
|---|---|---|---|---|---|---|---|---|---|---|
|  | 15 | 17 | 18 | 25 | 28 | 13 | 18 | 19 | 22 | 25 |
| Monday |  |  |  |  |  |  |  |  |  |  |
| Tuesday |  |  |  |  |  |  |  |  |  |  |
| Wednesday |  |  |  |  |  |  |  |  |  |  |
| Thursday |  |  |  |  |  |  |  |  |  |  |
| Friday |  |  |  |  |  |  |  |  |  |  |
| Study 13 |  |  |  |  |  |
| 18 |  |  |  |  |  |
| 19 |  |  |  |  |  |
| 22 |  |  |  |  |  |
| 25 |  |  |  |  |  |

| Evening | Sports | Study |
|---|---|---|
|  |  |  |
|  |  |  |
|  |  |  |
|  |  |  |
|  |  |  |

# Control Room

There are four monitors in the TV director's room, each
showing pictures from cameras trained on the lead cyclists
in this year's Crossways Cycle Race. Can you discover
who is pictured on each screen, the details of his bike, and
his current position? The plan of the monitors will help.

1 Bob Denny is two places behind the man on the silver bike, who
   is pictured on the monitor next to and right of that showing Tim
   Venton.

2 Guy Hartley is one place ahead of the man on the blue bike,
   who is pictured on the monitor directly above that showing Ron
   Summers.

3 The man on the green bike is one place behind the man whose
   picture appears on the monitor next to and right of that showing
   Guy Hartley.

|  | Cyclist | | | | Bike | | | | Position | | | |
|---|---|---|---|---|---|---|---|---|---|---|---|---|
|  | Bob Denny | Guy Hartley | Ron Summers | Tim Venton | Black | Blue | Green | Silver | First | Second | Third | Fourth |
| Monitor 1 | | | | | | | | | | | | |
| Monitor 2 | | | | | | | | | | | | |
| Monitor 3 | | | | | | | | | | | | |
| Monitor 4 | | | | | | | | | | | | |
| First | | | | | | | | | | | | |
| Second | | | | | | | | | | | | |
| Third | | | | | | | | | | | | |
| Fourth | | | | | | | | | | | | |
| Black | | | | | | | | | | | | |
| Blue | | | | | | | | | | | | |
| Green | | | | | | | | | | | | |
| Silver | | | | | | | | | | | | |

1    2

3    4

LEFT  RIGHT
⇐      ⇒

| Monitor | Cyclist | Bike | Position |
|---|---|---|---|
| | | | |
| | | | |
| | | | |
| | | | |

# Wedding Belles

In March 2018, Bella and her four bridesmaids made arrangements with different companies for her wedding, and left a deposit at each appointment. Use the clues and the calendar to determine which one of Bella's bridesmaids accompanied her each day, where they went, and the amount of deposit that was made.

1 Amy didn't accompany Bella on a Monday.
2 Lucy and Bella visited the catering company, where Bella left a larger deposit than she gave at the company she visited five days later.
3 Bella made her choice of flowers on the 14th, and she left $50 more at the florist's shop than she did at the hairdresser's salon.
4 Bella was accompanied by Elizabeth later in the month than the day on which she left a deposit of $125.

|  | Amy | Elizabeth | Lucy | Robina | Caterer | Florist | Hairdresser | Photographer | $100 | $125 | $150 | $175 |
|---|---|---|---|---|---|---|---|---|---|---|---|---|
| 5th |  |  |  |  |  |  |  |  |  |  |  |  |
| 9th |  |  |  |  |  |  |  |  |  |  |  |  |
| 14th |  |  |  |  |  |  |  |  |  |  |  |  |
| 19th |  |  |  |  |  |  |  |  |  |  |  |  |
| $100 |  |  |  |  |  |  |  |  | | | | |
| $125 |  |  |  |  |  |  |  |  | | | | |
| $150 |  |  |  |  |  |  |  |  | | | | |
| $175 |  |  |  |  |  |  |  |  | | | | |
| Caterer |  |  |  |  | | | | | | | | |
| Florist |  |  |  |  | | | | | | | | |
| Hairdresser |  |  |  |  | | | | | | | | |
| Photographer |  |  |  |  | | | | | | | | |

**MARCH**

| MON | TUES | WED | THUR | FRI | SAT | SUN |
|---|---|---|---|---|---|---|
|  |  |  | 1 | 2 | 3 | 4 |
| (5) | 6 | 7 | 8 | (9) | 10 | 11 |
| 12 | 13 | (14) | 15 | 16 | 17 | 18 |
| (19) | 20 | 21 | 22 | 23 | 24 | 25 |
| 26 | 27 | 28 | 29 | 30 | 31 |  |

| Date | Bridesmaid | Company | Deposit |
|---|---|---|---|
|  |  |  |  |
|  |  |  |  |
|  |  |  |  |
|  |  |  |  |

# Delegates in Dolbeau

Varying numbers of delegates from different countries descended on Dolbeau for their corporations' annual conferences last year. Each conference was held in a different month and was given a different title, reflecting the company's aims and aspirations. For each of these titles, therefore, can you work out the number of delegates who attended and their countries of origin?

1 Three more delegates attended the *Good For Us* conference than the number who attended the *Positive Thoughts* conference.

2 There was one fewer delegate from Austria than the number of delegates at the conference entitled *The Way Forward*.

3 *To the Future* was the title of the conference attended by two more delegates (not from Sweden) than the number who came from France.

4 Five more delegates attended the conference entitled *A New Direction* than the number who came from Norway.

|  | Delegates | | | | | Country | | | | |
|---|---|---|---|---|---|---|---|---|---|---|
|  | 15 | 16 | 18 | 20 | 21 | Austria | England | France | Norway | Sweden |
| A New Direction |  |  |  |  |  |  |  |  |  |  |
| Good for Us |  |  |  |  |  |  |  |  |  |  |
| Positive Thoughts |  |  |  |  |  |  |  |  |  |  |
| The Way Forward |  |  |  |  |  |  |  |  |  |  |
| To the Future |  |  |  |  |  |  |  |  |  |  |
| Austria |  |  |  |  |  |
| England |  |  |  |  |  |
| France |  |  |  |  |  |
| Norway |  |  |  |  |  |
| Sweden |  |  |  |  |  |

| Conference | Delegates | Country |
|---|---|---|
|  |  |  |
|  |  |  |
|  |  |  |
|  |  |  |
|  |  |  |

# Taking Care of the Pets

Wendy is emigrating abroad next year, and cannot take her pets with her. Luckily some of her friends and relatives have asked if they could adopt them, so Wendy is overjoyed to have found good homes for them all. What type of creature is each of the named pets, and for how long have they enjoyed Wendy's affection?

1 Bobby isn't the canary, which has been with Wendy for four fewer months than Lola.

2 Dilly the dog has been with Wendy for six months longer than the hamster (who hasn't been with Wendy for ten months).

3 Kandy has lived with Wendy for longer than the rabbit.

4 Kandy isn't Wendy's cat.

| | Type | | | | | Time | | | | |
| --- | --- | --- | --- | --- | --- | --- | --- | --- | --- | --- |
| | Canary | Cat | Dog | Hamster | Rabbit | 6 months | 10 months | 12 months | 16 months | 18 months |
| Bobby | | | | | | | | | | |
| Dilly | | | | | | | | | | |
| Kandy | | | | | | | | | | |
| Lola | | | | | | | | | | |
| Midge | | | | | | | | | | |
| 6 months | | | | | | | | | | |
| 10 months | | | | | | | | | | |
| 12 months | | | | | | | | | | |
| 16 months | | | | | | | | | | |
| 18 months | | | | | | | | | | |

| Pet | Type | Time |
| --- | --- | --- |
| | | |
| | | |
| | | |
| | | |
| | | |

# Musically Minded

Four friends each play a different musical instrument, and prefers the work of a different composer (not necessarily one who wrote music associated with the instrument he or she plays). Discover each friend's full name, the instrument he or she plays, and the preferred composer of each, by using the clues below.

1 The person who prefers the music of Debussy doesn't play the oboe and isn't named Hale. The person whose last name is Hale doesn't play the oboe or the clarinet.

2 Henry's last name is Forbes. He doesn't play the oboe.

3 The person who plays the viola prefers the work of Elgar, unlike Florence, whose preferred composer isn't Mahler.

4 Albert (whose last name isn't Dexter) plays the clarinet. Florence's last name isn't Dexter.

|  | Last name | | | | Instrument | | | | Composer | | | |
|---|---|---|---|---|---|---|---|---|---|---|---|---|
|  | Dexter | Forbes | Hale | Price | Clarinet | Oboe | Piano | Viola | Debussy | Elgar | Mahler | Wagner |
| Albert |  |  |  |  |  |  |  |  |  |  |  |  |
| Florence |  |  |  |  |  |  |  |  |  |  |  |  |
| Henry |  |  |  |  |  |  |  |  |  |  |  |  |  |
| Sophie |  |  |  |  |  |  |  |  |  |  |  |  |  |
| Debussy |  |  |  |  |  |  |  |  |  |  |  |  |  |
| Elgar |  |  |  |  |  |  |  |  |  |  |  |  |  |
| Mahler |  |  |  |  |  |  |  |  |  |  |  |  |  |
| Wagner |  |  |  |  |  |  |  |  |  |  |  |  |  |
| Clarinet |  |  |  |  |  |  |  |  |  |  |  |  |  |
| Oboe |  |  |  |  |  |  |  |  |  |  |  |  |  |
| Piano |  |  |  |  |  |  |  |  |  |  |  |  |  |
| Viola |  |  |  |  |  |  |  |  |  |  |  |  |  |

| Name | Last name | Instrument | Composer |
|---|---|---|---|
|  |  |  |  |
|  |  |  |  |
|  |  |  |  |
|  |  |  |  |

# Nice Nails

Noreen runs a small business, Nice Nails, from home and had four customers yesterday afternoon, each booked for a manicure and nail polishing session. Can you discover each customer's full name, the time of her appointment, and the nail polish she chose?

1 Noreen's first customer of the afternoon was Mrs Nixon, who chose Coffee Cream polish.

2 Nancy's appointment was earlier than that of Nerys. Nancy's last name isn't Nugent.

3 The Violent Violet nail polish was chosen by the woman whose appointment was one and a half hours earlier than Nona's.

4 Naomi's appointment was one and a half hours earlier than that of Miss Neame (who isn't Nona and didn't choose the Rowdy Red nail polish).

| | Last name | | | | Time | | | | Polish | | | |
|---|---|---|---|---|---|---|---|---|---|---|---|---|
| | Neame | Nixon | Norris | Nugent | 2.00pm | 2.45pm | 3.30pm | 4.15pm | Coffee Cream | Perfect Pink | Rowdy Red | Violent Violet |
| Nancy | | | | | | | | | | | | |
| Naomi | | | | | | | | | | | | |
| Nerys | | | | | | | | | | | | |
| Nona | | | | | | | | | | | | |
| Coffee Cream | | | | | | | | | | | | |
| Perfect Pink | | | | | | | | | | | | |
| Rowdy Red | | | | | | | | | | | | |
| Violent Violet | | | | | | | | | | | | |
| 2.00pm | | | | | | | | | | | | |
| 2.45pm | | | | | | | | | | | | |
| 3.30pm | | | | | | | | | | | | |
| 4.15pm | | | | | | | | | | | | |

| Customer | Last name | Time | Polish |
|---|---|---|---|
| | | | |
| | | | |
| | | | |
| | | | |

# Childcare Costs

Five women attended different business functions last Tuesday evening, and had to hire babysitters to look after the children. When they met up for coffee yesterday morning, the women compared notes on the costs charged by the various babysitters. You can also work out the details relating to each woman in terms of the hourly rate she paid, and the number of hours for which the babysitter was hired.

1 The babysitter who charged $7 per hour worked for two hours longer than the one who charged $5 per hour.

2 Diane's babysitter charged $10 per hour.

3 The babysitter hired for the shortest time charged either $5 per hour more or $5 per hour less than Chloë's babysitter.

4 Thelma's babysitter charged $15 per hour, and her total bill for the evening was double Diane's.

5 Gill's total bill for the evening was higher than Rose's total bill.

|  | No of hours | | | | | Hourly rate | | | | |
|---|---|---|---|---|---|---|---|---|---|---|
|  | 3 | 4 | 5 | 6 | 7 | $5 | $7 | $8 | $10 | $15 |
| Chloë |  |  |  |  |  |  |  |  |  |  |
| Diane |  |  |  |  |  |  |  |  |  |  |
| Gill |  |  |  |  |  |  |  |  |  |  |
| Rose |  |  |  |  |  |  |  |  |  |  |
| Thelma |  |  |  |  |  |  |  |  |  |  |
| $5 |  |  |  |  |  |
| $7 |  |  |  |  |  |
| $8 |  |  |  |  |  |
| $10 |  |  |  |  |  |
| $15 |  |  |  |  |  |

Hourly rate

| Woman | Hours | Rate |
|---|---|---|
|  |  |  |
|  |  |  |
|  |  |  |
|  |  |  |
|  |  |  |

# Holey Works

The Museum of Modern Sculpture has a small area in the lobby which is devoted to the work of abstract sculptor Ivor Chiselle of the Holey Works Studio. From the clues and diagram below (which shows his most recent pieces), can you name each piece, and determine the month and year in which it was completed?

1 The piece entitled *Anger* has one more hole than that completed in August 2005, but one fewer hole than Ivor Chiselle's most recent creation.

2 The work completed three months later than *Jealousy* is next to and further right than *Jealousy*.

3 *Revenge* was completed earlier than *Sorrow*, but later than *Fury*.

4 Piece C was completed some time during 2005.

|  | Title | | | | | Completed | | | | |
|---|---|---|---|---|---|---|---|---|---|---|
|  | Anger | Fury | Jealousy | Revenge | Sorrow | May 2005 | August 2005 | May 2006 | August 2006 | December 06 |
| Piece A |  |  |  |  |  |  |  |  |  |  |
| Piece B |  |  |  |  |  |  |  |  |  |  |
| Piece C |  |  |  |  |  |  |  |  |  |  |
| Piece D |  |  |  |  |  |  |  |  |  |  |
| Piece E |  |  |  |  |  |  |  |  |  |  |
| May 2005 |  |  |  |  |  |  |  |  |  |  |
| August 2005 |  |  |  |  |  |  |  |  |  |  |
| May 2006 |  |  |  |  |  |  |  |  |  |  |
| August 2006 |  |  |  |  |  |  |  |  |  |  |
| December 2006 |  |  |  |  |  |  |  |  |  |  |

**LEFT** ⇦    **RIGHT** ⇨

A  B

C  D  E

| Piece | Title | Completed |
|---|---|---|
|  |  |  |
|  |  |  |
|  |  |  |
|  |  |  |
|  |  |  |

# Flower Power

Business is blooming at Flora's Flower Shop. Her first four customers this morning each bought a huge bouquet of a particular type of flower. Can you discover the full names of the first four customers, the type of flowers each bought, and the order in which they were served?

1 Mrs Moor was served immediately before the customer who bought carnations, but later than Rowan.

2 Mr Grove bought two dozen of Flora's finest long-stem roses.

3 Herb was served earlier than the customer who bought a large bunch of mixed lilies, but later than the customer named Bedding.

4 Ivy wasn't the third customer to be served.

|  | Last name | | | | Flowers | | | | Order | | | |
|---|---|---|---|---|---|---|---|---|---|---|---|---|
|  | Bedding | Grove | Hill | Moor | Asters | Carnations | Lilies | Roses | First | Second | Third | Fourth |
| Daisy |  |  |  |  |  |  |  |  |  |  |  |  |
| Herb |  |  |  |  |  |  |  |  |  |  |  |  |
| Ivy |  |  |  |  |  |  |  |  |  |  |  |  |
| Rowan |  |  |  |  |  |  |  |  |  |  |  |  |
| First |  |  |  |  |  |  |  |  | | | | |
| Second |  |  |  |  |  |  |  |  | | | | |
| Third |  |  |  |  |  |  |  |  | | | | |
| Fourth |  |  |  |  |  |  |  |  | | | | |
| Asters |  |  |  |  | | | | | | | | |
| Carnations |  |  |  |  | | | | | | | | |
| Lilies |  |  |  |  | | | | | | | | |
| Roses |  |  |  |  | | | | | | | | |

| Name | Last name | Flowers | Order |
|---|---|---|---|
|  |  |  |  |
|  |  |  |  |
|  |  |  |  |
|  |  |  |  |

# Family Holidays

The four families who feature in this puzzle have escaped city life by renting beach houses. Can you discover the name of the husband and wife in each family, discover how many children they have, and say which town they are from?

1 Sally and her husband have one more child than Neil and his wife, and two more children than the couple from Whitvale.

2 Dan and his wife have one more child than the couple from Middleton, and two more children than Nerys and her husband.

3 The couple from Eastville have one more child than Debbie and her husband, and two more children than Fred and his wife.

4 Mark and his wife are from Colwood, and have more than two children.

|  | Wife | | | | Children | | | | Town | | | |
|---|---|---|---|---|---|---|---|---|---|---|---|---|
|  | Debbie | Heather | Nerys | Sally | 2 | 3 | 4 | 5 | Colwood | Eastville | Middleton | Whitvale |
| Dan |  |  |  |  |  |  |  |  |  |  |  |  |
| Fred |  |  |  |  |  |  |  |  |  |  |  |  |
| Mark |  |  |  |  |  |  |  |  |  |  |  |  |
| Neil |  |  |  |  |  |  |  |  |  |  |  |  |
| Colwood |  |  |  |  |  |  |  |  |  |  |  |  |
| Eastville |  |  |  |  |  |  |  |  |  |  |  |  |
| Middleton |  |  |  |  |  |  |  |  |  |  |  |  |
| Whitvale |  |  |  |  |  |  |  |  |  |  |  |  |
| 2 children |  |  |  |  |  |  |  |  |  |  |  |  |
| 3 children |  |  |  |  |  |  |  |  |  |  |  |  |
| 4 children |  |  |  |  |  |  |  |  |  |  |  |  |
| 5 children |  |  |  |  |  |  |  |  |  |  |  |  |

| Husband | Wife | Children | Town |
|---|---|---|---|
|  |  |  |  |
|  |  |  |  |
|  |  |  |  |
|  |  |  |  |

# At the Crossroads

The plan below shows the position of five houses at the crossroads near the village of Ruralton. Can you name each house and its resident, by following the clues?

1 Apple Lodge is directly east of High View.

2 Mr Upton lives further east than Miss Soul (whose home is The Willows) and further north than Mrs Walters.

3 Mrs Vane lives in Daleside, which is further east and further south than Rose House.

|  | Name | | | | | Resident | | | | |
|---|---|---|---|---|---|---|---|---|---|---|
|  | Apple Lodge | Daleside | High View | Rose House | The Willows | Miss Soul | Mr Trimble | Mr Upton | Mrs Vane | Mrs Walters |
| No 1 |  |  |  |  |  |  |  |  |  |  |
| No 2 |  |  |  |  |  |  |  |  |  |  |
| No 3 |  |  |  |  |  |  |  |  |  |  |
| No 4 |  |  |  |  |  |  |  |  |  |  |
| No 5 |  |  |  |  |  |  |  |  |  |  |
| Miss Soul |  |  |  |  |  |
| Mr Trimble |  |  |  |  |  |
| Mr Upton |  |  |  |  |  |
| Mrs Vane |  |  |  |  |  |
| Mrs Walters |  |  |  |  |  |

| House No | Name | Resident |
|---|---|---|
|  |  |  |
|  |  |  |
|  |  |  |
|  |  |  |
|  |  |  |

# Housework

Brendan hadn't thought about housework until his friends, parents, and other visitors to his apartment encouraged him to do so! Over the course of five evenings last week, he spent time on a particular task which badly needed to be done. How much time did he devote to each task, and on which evening of the week was it done?

1 Brendan tidied his apartment the day before he did the dusting (which took him twice as long as the laundry).

2 The laundry was done two days before the ironing, but later in the week than the task which had taken Brendan the longest time to complete.

3 The vacuuming took Brendan less time than Friday's job.

4 The job done on Friday took an hour longer than the job done on Tuesday.

|  | Time | | | | | Day | | | | |
|---|---|---|---|---|---|---|---|---|---|---|
|  | 1 hour | 1½ hours | 2 hours | 3 hours | 3½ hours | Monday | Tuesday | Wednesday | Thursday | Friday |
| Dusting |  |  |  |  |  |  |  |  |  |  |
| Ironing |  |  |  |  |  |  |  |  |  |  |
| Laundry |  |  |  |  |  |  |  |  |  |  |
| Tidying |  |  |  |  |  |  |  |  |  |  |
| Vacuuming |  |  |  |  |  |  |  |  |  |  |
| Monday |  |  |  |  |  |
| Tuesday |  |  |  |  |  |
| Wednesday |  |  |  |  |  |
| Thursday |  |  |  |  |  |
| Friday |  |  |  |  |  |

| Task | Time | Day |
|---|---|---|
|  |  |  |
|  |  |  |
|  |  |  |
|  |  |  |
|  |  |  |

# The Book Club

Marilyn has four books on the top shelf of her room divider. Can you discover the title and author of each, together with its year of publication, by following the clues and studying the picture below?

1  The book by P Hubbard is further right than *The Clock*, but further left than at least one other book.

2  The book published in 1987 is directly next to and left of *Forever*.

3  The novel by S Willis was published twelve years later than book C.

4  The book by M Potter is directly next to and left of *Summer Joy*, which wasn't written by J Barnes.

5  The book by J Barnes is further left than *Jo's Sons*, but further right than at least one other book.

|  | Title | | | | Author | | | | Year | | | |
|---|---|---|---|---|---|---|---|---|---|---|---|---|
|  | The Clock | Forever | Jo's Sons | Summer Joy | J Barnes | P Hubbard | M Potter | S Willis | 1987 | 1993 | 1999 | 2005 |
| Book A |  |  |  |  |  |  |  |  |  |  |  |  |
| Book B |  |  |  |  |  |  |  |  |  |  |  |  |
| Book C |  |  |  |  |  |  |  |  |  |  |  |  |
| Book D |  |  |  |  |  |  |  |  |  |  |  |  |
| 1987 |  |  |  |  |  |  |  |  |
| 1993 |  |  |  |  |  |  |  |  |
| 1999 |  |  |  |  |  |  |  |  |
| 2005 |  |  |  |  |  |  |  |  |
| J Barnes |  |  |  |  |
| P Hubbard |  |  |  |  |
| M Potter |  |  |  |  |
| S Willis |  |  |  |  |

LEFT ⇦   RIGHT ⇨

A B C D

| Book | Title | Author | Year |
|---|---|---|---|
|  |  |  |  |
|  |  |  |  |
|  |  |  |  |
|  |  |  |  |

# Bargains

The diagram below shows four people who took a table at yesterday's Church Sale. At exactly eleven o'clock every one of the four table holders made their tenth sale of the day! Can you identify each table holder and his or her customer, and say which item of bric-à-brac was being sold at the time?

1  Marcus didn't buy anything from Doreen, who is furthest left in the diagram below.

2  Joanne (who didn't buy anything from Neil) was the customer of person C.

3  Person B sold a coffee pot at eleven o'clock yesterday morning.

4  One person stood between James (who sold something to Andy) and the table holder who sold the watering can.

5  Martina isn't the table holder who sold the full-length mirror.

| | Table holder | | | | Buyer | | | | Item | | | |
|---|---|---|---|---|---|---|---|---|---|---|---|---|
| | Doreen | James | Martina | Neil | Andy | Joanne | Lucy | Marcus | Coffee pot | Mirror | Toaster | Watering can |
| Person A | | | | | | | | | | | | |
| Person B | | | | | | | | | | | | |
| Person C | | | | | | | | | | | | |
| Person D | | | | | | | | | | | | |
| Coffee pot | | | | | | | | | | | | |
| Mirror | | | | | | | | | | | | |
| Toaster | | | | | | | | | | | | |
| Watering can | | | | | | | | | | | | |
| Andy | | | | | | | | | | | | |
| Joanne | | | | | | | | | | | | |
| Lucy | | | | | | | | | | | | |
| Marcus | | | | | | | | | | | | |

LEFT ⇦          RIGHT ⇨

A  B  C  D

| Person | Table holder | Buyer | Item |
|---|---|---|---|
| | | | |
| | | | |
| | | | |
| | | | |

# Animal Art

After a visit to the zoo, Mrs Brown's five children all painted a picture of the animals they liked best. They couldn't remember exactly what the animals look like in real life, so each child painted the animal in the shade he or she likes best, which made for some rather interesting pictures! Can you discover every child's preferences?

1 Amy painted the giraffe and one of her brothers painted the red mongoose.
2 Christopher used purple paint and one of his brothers used liberal quantities of lime green.
3 Daniel painted the chimpanzee.
4 Marina didn't paint the aardvark and didn't use any orange paint.

|  | Aardvark | Chimpanzee | Elephant | Giraffe | Mongoose | Blue | Green | Orange | Purple | Red |
|---|---|---|---|---|---|---|---|---|---|---|
| Amy | | | | | | | | | | |
| Christopher | | | | | | | | | | |
| Daniel | | | | | | | | | | |
| Marina | | | | | | | | | | |
| Rory | | | | | | | | | | |
| Blue | | | | | | | | | | |
| Green | | | | | | | | | | |
| Orange | | | | | | | | | | |
| Purple | | | | | | | | | | |
| Red | | | | | | | | | | |

| Child | Animal | Paint |
|---|---|---|
| | | |
| | | |
| | | |
| | | |
| | | |

# Photographic Memories

On top of her bookcase, Alice has five photographs taken on her various vacations over the years. Can you discover the country and date in which each photograph was taken? A plan of the line-up of the photographs is shown below.

1 The photograph taken by Alice when she was on holiday in England is larger than the picture taken in 2000.

2 The picture taken in 2000 is directly next to and right of the one she took when on holiday the year before she went to Spain.

3 The picture from Alice's holiday in Sweden was taken two years later than photograph E in the plan below.

4 Alice holidayed in Canada three years after she went to Germany.

5 The picture taken in 2004 is directly next to and left of that taken in 2003.

|  | Canada | England | Germany | Spain | Sweden | 2000 | 2002 | 2003 | 2004 | 2006 |
|---|---|---|---|---|---|---|---|---|---|---|
| Photo A |  |  |  |  |  |  |  |  |  |  |
| Photo B |  |  |  |  |  |  |  |  |  |  |
| Photo C |  |  |  |  |  |  |  |  |  |  |
| Photo D |  |  |  |  |  |  |  |  |  |  |
| Photo E |  |  |  |  |  |  |  |  |  |  |
| 2000 |  |  |  |  |  | | | | | |
| 2002 |  |  |  |  |  | | | | | |
| 2003 |  |  |  |  |  | | | | | |
| 2004 |  |  |  |  |  | | | | | |
| 2006 |  |  |  |  |  | | | | | |

**LEFT** ⇦          **RIGHT** ⇨

A  B  C  D  E

| Photo | Country | Year |
|---|---|---|
|  |  |  |
|  |  |  |
|  |  |  |
|  |  |  |
|  |  |  |

# Can Display

Marian's store cupboard contains twelve cans of fruit, and she has three cans of the four different fruits listed in the grid below. On each of the three shelves (as per the diagram) there are four cans with different contents, so every fruit appears just once per shelf. Can you correctly identify them all?

**1** Each fruit is in cans identified by three different letters.

**2** On the top shelf, the cherries are further right than their position on the bottom shelf (where they are next to and right of a can of pears).

**3** On the top shelf, the pears are next to and right of a can of plums.

**4** On the top shelf, the lychees are further right than their position on the bottom shelf. They are not in can A on the middle shelf.

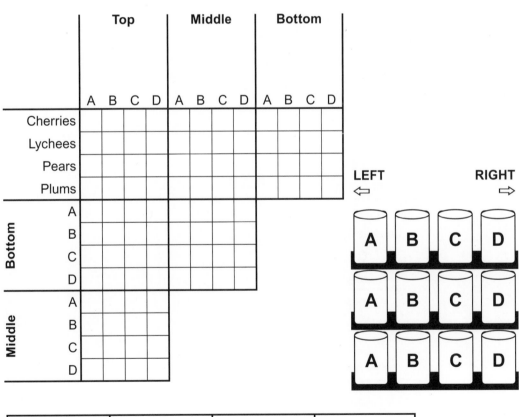

| Fruit | Top | Middle | Bottom |
|-------|-----|--------|--------|
|       |     |        |        |
|       |     |        |        |
|       |     |        |        |
|       |     |        |        |

# Dazzling Dancers

Four girls went out last Saturday night with their boyfriends, each to a different club in town. The girls each wore sequined tops in different shades. Can you discover the name of each one's boyfriend, the details of the top worn by each girl, and the name of the club in which each couple danced the night away?

1  Barbara wouldn't be seen dead in gold, nor in the purple top that Norman's girlfriend wore – last year's shade according to Barbara.

2  Colin and his girlfriend (not Rachel) went to Laramie's.

3  The girl who wore the gold top danced at the Texada club.

4  Shona and her boyfriend danced at QC.

5  Rachel wore a sequined silver top.

6  Jackie's boyfriend is Dave.

|  | \multicolumn{4}{Boyfriend} | \multicolumn{4}{Top} | \multicolumn{4}{Club} |
|---|---|---|---|---|---|---|---|---|---|---|---|---|
|  | Colin | Dave | Norman | Pete | Gold | Pink | Purple | Silver | Blue Lagoon | Laramie's | QC | Texada |
| Barbara |  |  |  |  |  |  |  |  |  |  |  |  |
| Jackie |  |  |  |  |  |  |  |  |  |  |  |  |
| Rachel |  |  |  |  |  |  |  |  |  |  |  |  |
| Shona |  |  |  |  |  |  |  |  |  |  |  |  |
| Blue Lagoon |  |  |  |  |  |  |  |  | | | | |
| Laramie's |  |  |  |  |  |  |  |  | | | | |
| QC |  |  |  |  |  |  |  |  | | | | |
| Texada |  |  |  |  |  |  |  |  | | | | |
| Gold |  |  |  |  | | | | | | | | |
| Pink |  |  |  |  | | | | | | | | |
| Purple |  |  |  |  | | | | | | | | |
| Silver |  |  |  |  | | | | | | | | |

| Girl | Boyfriend | Top | Club |
|---|---|---|---|
|  |  |  |  |
|  |  |  |  |
|  |  |  |  |
|  |  |  |  |

The first five people have begun to set up their tables for the Middleton Craft Fair which begins later today. Can you discover the number of each woman's table, and the type of goods she will be displaying for sale?

1  Gail makes a wide selection of necklaces, and is setting up a table with a higher number than that on which the pottery will be displayed. Ariadne does not make pottery.

2  Sandra (who isn't at table number 10) has a selection of still life oil paintings to sell.

3  Pauline is at table number 12, and the knitwear is being laid out on table number 16.

4  Megan is neither the woman who owns a loom and makes woven goods, nor the one who makes pottery.

|  | Table No | | | | | Goods | | | | |
|---|---|---|---|---|---|---|---|---|---|---|
|  | 10 | 11 | 12 | 16 | 17 | Knitwear | Necklaces | Paintings | Pottery | Woven goods |
| Ariadne |  |  |  |  |  |  |  |  |  |  |
| Gail |  |  |  |  |  |  |  |  |  |  |
| Megan |  |  |  |  |  |  |  |  |  |  |
| Pauline |  |  |  |  |  |  |  |  |  |  |
| Sandra |  |  |  |  |  |  |  |  |  |  |
| Knitwear |  |  |  |  |  |
| Necklaces |  |  |  |  |  |
| Paintings |  |  |  |  |  |
| Pottery |  |  |  |  |  |
| Woven goods |  |  |  |  |  |

| Name | Table No | Goods |
|---|---|---|
|  |  |  |
|  |  |  |
|  |  |  |
|  |  |  |
|  |  |  |

# Racing Wrecks

The men who appear in this puzzle all enjoy racing old cars around a track. In their latest race, all of the cars managed to finish, despite developing problems after a few laps of the track. Can you discover with which part of his car each driver experienced a problem, together with the position in which he finished the race?

1  Carl finished more than one place further ahead than the man who experienced a problem with the accelerator pedal, but further behind than the one whose radiator sprang a leak.
2  The man whose steering became erratic had to slow his speed, but still managed to get to the finishing line before Joe.
3  Marc finished two places behind the driver whose brakes temporarily jammed.
4  Phil finished in fourth position.
5  Hal had no problem with his radiator.

|  | Accelerator | Brakes | Clutch | Radiator | Steering | First | Second | Third | Fourth | Fifth |
|---|---|---|---|---|---|---|---|---|---|---|
| Carl |  |  |  |  |  |  |  |  |  |  |
| Hal |  |  |  |  |  |  |  |  |  |  |
| Joe |  |  |  |  |  |  |  |  |  |  |
| Marc |  |  |  |  |  |  |  |  |  |  |
| Phil |  |  |  |  |  |  |  |  |  |  |
| First |  |  |  |  |  |
| Second |  |  |  |  |  |
| Third |  |  |  |  |  |
| Fourth |  |  |  |  |  |
| Fifth |  |  |  |  |  |

| Driver | Part | Position |
|---|---|---|
|  |  |  |
|  |  |  |
|  |  |  |
|  |  |  |
|  |  |  |

# Truck Stop

Four trucks are currently waiting at traffic lights before
they can continue on their respective journeys. Can
you discover who is driving each truck in the line-up,
together with his load, and the name of the town to which
he is going? Quick… before the lights change!

1 Burt is going to Foxburgh. He's further back in the line-up than
the truck loaded with onions, but further forward in the line-up
than the man journeying to Capfield.

2 Dick is one place further back in the line-up than the truck laden
with cans of dog food.

3 Lance's truck is carrying boxes of detergent, and is further
forward in the line-up than the one heading towards Pitbury.

|  | Driver | | | | Load | | | | Town | | | |
|---|---|---|---|---|---|---|---|---|---|---|---|---|
|  | Burt | Dick | Jeremy | Lance | Detergent | Dog food | Footwear | Onions | Baywood | Capfield | Foxburgh | Pitbury |
| First |  |  |  |  |  |  |  |  |  |  |  |  |
| Second |  |  |  |  |  |  |  |  |  |  |  |  |
| Third |  |  |  |  |  |  |  |  |  |  |  |  |
| Fourth |  |  |  |  |  |  |  |  |  |  |  |  |
| Baywood |  |  |  |  |  |  |  |  |  |  |  |  |
| Capfield |  |  |  |  |  |  |  |  |  |  |  |  |
| Foxburgh |  |  |  |  |  |  |  |  |  |  |  |  |
| Pitbury |  |  |  |  |  |  |  |  |  |  |  |  |
| Detergent |  |  |  |  |  |  |  |  |  |  |  |  |
| Dog food |  |  |  |  |  |  |  |  |  |  |  |  |
| Footwear |  |  |  |  |  |  |  |  |  |  |  |  |
| Onions |  |  |  |  |  |  |  |  |  |  |  |  |

1st  2nd  3rd  4th

| Position | Driver | Load | Town |
|---|---|---|---|
|  |  |  |  |
|  |  |  |  |
|  |  |  |  |
|  |  |  |  |

# Happy Birthday

Four teenage friends are celebrating birthdays next week. Use the clues below to discover each one's full name, the day on which he or she has a birthday, and his or her current age.

1 Frank is two years older than the person named Vaughn, whose birthday is two days earlier than Michael's.
2 Jane's last name is Jenkins.
3 Lucy's birthday is the day after that of the 16-year-old, but the day before that of the person named Milton, who isn't the oldest of the four friends.
4 The person named Connor celebrates a birthday next Thursday.

| | Last name | | | | Day | | | | Age | | | |
|---|---|---|---|---|---|---|---|---|---|---|---|---|
| | Connor | Jenkins | Milton | Vaughn | Monday | Tuesday | Wednesday | Thursday | 15 | 16 | 17 | 18 |
| Frank | | | | | | | | | | | | |
| Jane | | | | | | | | | | | | |
| Lucy | | | | | | | | | | | | |
| Michael | | | | | | | | | | | | |
| 15 years old | | | | | | | | | | | | |
| 16 years old | | | | | | | | | | | | |
| 17 years old | | | | | | | | | | | | |
| 18 years old | | | | | | | | | | | | |
| Monday | | | | | | | | | | | | |
| Tuesday | | | | | | | | | | | | |
| Wednesday | | | | | | | | | | | | |
| Thursday | | | | | | | | | | | | |

| Name | Last name | Day | Age |
|---|---|---|---|
| | | | |
| | | | |
| | | | |
| | | | |

# Housing Problem

The five people in this puzzle all reside in the houses shown on the map below. Can you match first names to last names and point out where each person lives?

1  Jack lives directly east of the person named Finch.
2  Dolly lives further south than the person named Kingsley, who lives directly east of George.
3  Ingrid lives directly east of the person named Cooper.
4  The resident named Walsh lives further west than the one named Tate.
5  The number of the house in which Ella lives is not one lower than the number of the house in which the person named Cooper lives.

|  | First name | | | | | Last name | | | | |
|---|---|---|---|---|---|---|---|---|---|---|
|  | Dolly | Ella | George | Ingrid | Jack | Cooper | Finch | Kingsley | Tate | Walsh |
| House 1 |  |  |  |  |  |  |  |  |  |  |
| House 2 |  |  |  |  |  |  |  |  |  |  |
| House 3 |  |  |  |  |  |  |  |  |  |  |
| House 4 |  |  |  |  |  |  |  |  |  |  |
| House 5 |  |  |  |  |  |  |  |  |  |  |
| Cooper |  |  |  |  |  |  |  |  |  |  |
| Finch |  |  |  |  |  |  |  |  |  |  |
| Kingsley |  |  |  |  |  |  |  |  |  |  |
| Tate |  |  |  |  |  |  |  |  |  |  |
| Walsh |  |  |  |  |  |  |  |  |  |  |

N W E S

1

2   3

4   5

| House | First name | Last name |
|---|---|---|
|  |  |  |
|  |  |  |
|  |  |  |
|  |  |  |
|  |  |  |

# Where in the World?

The five people who feature in this puzzle took not one,
but two vacations last year, both in different countries.
Which country did each visit first and second?

1 Martin journeyed to Mauritius, Lynda to Jamaica, and Joseph to Italy.

2 Abigail holidayed in Ireland, but not in Israel.

3 No-one went to both Spain and Jamaica.

4 One of the five people went to both Canada and Brazil.

|  | First | | | | | Second | | | | |
|---|---|---|---|---|---|---|---|---|---|---|
|  | Canada | Israel | Jamaica | Jordan | Mauritius | Brazil | France | Ireland | Italy | Spain |
| Abigail |  |  |  |  |  |  |  |  |  |  |
| Joseph |  |  |  |  |  |  |  |  |  |  |
| Lynda |  |  |  |  |  |  |  |  |  |  |
| Martin |  |  |  |  |  |  |  |  |  |  |
| Stuart |  |  |  |  |  |  |  |  |  |  |
| Brazil |  |  |  |  |  |  |  |  |  |  |
| France |  |  |  |  |  |  |  |  |  |  |
| Ireland |  |  |  |  |  |  |  |  |  |  |
| Italy |  |  |  |  |  |  |  |  |  |  |
| Spain |  |  |  |  |  |  |  |  |  |  |

| Name | First | Second |
|---|---|---|
|  |  |  |
|  |  |  |
|  |  |  |
|  |  |  |
|  |  |  |

# Aliases

In 1926, passengers in four sleeping compartments on a train decided to travel incognito. Who occupied each numbered compartment, what name had each adopted for the trip, and why did he or she want to travel under a false identity?

1. Each passenger used a name appropriate to his or her sex.
2. The passenger in compartment 7 wasn't the man trying to escape from his domineering wife for a few days.
3. "Kate Thomas" was in a carriage with a higher number than that taken by the passenger who was to attend a secret meeting.
4. Lady Jones was carrying a large quantity of jewels on the trip, and did not want to draw attention to herself.
5. The Duc d'Auvil had a compartment with a number one lower than that of Prince Paul, who was eloping.
6. "Sara Brown" didn't occupy a compartment with a number two lower than that taken by the one calling himself "Bill Smith".

|  | Real name | | | | Alias | | | | Reason | | | |
|---|---|---|---|---|---|---|---|---|---|---|---|---|
|  | Duc D'Auvil | Lady Jones | Queen Jane | Prince Paul | Bill Smith | Kate Thomas | Oscar Lane | Sara Brown | Carrying jewels | Eloping | Escaping wife | Secret meeting |
| Compartment 4 |  |  |  |  |  |  |  |  |  |  |  |  |
| Compartment 6 |  |  |  |  |  |  |  |  |  |  |  |  |
| Compartment 7 |  |  |  |  |  |  |  |  |  |  |  |  |
| Compartment 8 |  |  |  |  |  |  |  |  |  |  |  |  |
| Carrying jewels |  |  |  |  |  |  |  |  |  |  |  |  |
| Eloping |  |  |  |  |  |  |  |  |  |  |  |  |
| Escaping wife |  |  |  |  |  |  |  |  |  |  |  |  |
| Secret meeting |  |  |  |  |  |  |  |  |  |  |  |  |
| Bill Smith |  |  |  |  |  |  |  |  |  |  |  |  |
| K Thomas |  |  |  |  |  |  |  |  |  |  |  |  |
| Oscar Lane |  |  |  |  |  |  |  |  |  |  |  |  |
| Sara Brown |  |  |  |  |  |  |  |  |  |  |  |  |

| Compartment | Real name | Alias | Reason |
|---|---|---|---|
|  |  |  |  |
|  |  |  |  |
|  |  |  |  |
|  |  |  |  |

# Chess Master

**60**

Keith Knight has just become the youngest-ever Canadian chess grandmaster, having left a trail of opponents defeated in a series of matches across the country. From the following clues, can you discover the name of his rival in each city, the time taken to play each game, and the amount of prize money won by Keith?

1  Keith beat Kevin King (although not in Vancouver) in twenty minutes less time than it took to crush his opponent in Calgary.

2  As a result of the game in Calgary, Keith won more than he had taken for winning a match in forty minutes. At neither of these two games was his opponent Bill Bishop.

3  The game which netted Keith a prize of $250 took twenty minutes longer than the match against Raymond Rook.

4  More money was won by Keith in Vancouver than in Winnipeg; and more money was won by Keith in Winnipeg than in Edmonton.

|  | Bill Bishop | Kevin King | Quentin Queen | Raymond Rook | 40 minutes | 50 minutes | 70 minutes | 90 minutes | $250 | $350 | $450 | $550 |
|---|---|---|---|---|---|---|---|---|---|---|---|---|
| Calgary |  |  |  |  |  |  |  |  |  |  |  |  |
| Edmonton |  |  |  |  |  |  |  |  |  |  |  |  |
| Vancouver |  |  |  |  |  |  |  |  |  |  |  |  |
| Winnipeg |  |  |  |  |  |  |  |  |  |  |  |  |
| $250 |  |  |  |  |  |  |  |  |  |  |  |  |
| $350 |  |  |  |  |  |  |  |  |  |  |  |  |
| $450 |  |  |  |  |  |  |  |  |  |  |  |  |
| $550 |  |  |  |  |  |  |  |  |  |  |  |  |
| 40 minutes |  |  |  |  |  |  |  |  |  |  |  |  |
| 50 minutes |  |  |  |  |  |  |  |  |  |  |  |  |
| 70 minutes |  |  |  |  |  |  |  |  |  |  |  |  |
| 90 minutes |  |  |  |  |  |  |  |  |  |  |  |  |

| City | Opponent | Time | Prize |
|---|---|---|---|
|  |  |  |  |
|  |  |  |  |
|  |  |  |  |
|  |  |  |  |

# Pippa's Pictures

Pippa has pictures of five of her relatives, each hanging in a frame on her bedroom wall. Who is the subject of each picture, and what is his or her relationship to Pippa?

1 Donald's picture is higher and further left than that of Pippa's daughter.

2 Luke's picture has a number one higher than that of Magda. Magda's picture is further left than that of Pippa's brother.

3 The picture of Pippa's brother has a higher number than that of her mother, but a lower number than that of Pauline, whose picture is further left than that of Pippa's cousin.

|  | Subject | | | | | Relationship | | | | |
|---|---|---|---|---|---|---|---|---|---|---|
|  | Donald | Kirsty | Luke | Magda | Pauline | Brother | Cousin | Daughter | Mother | Uncle |
| Picture 1 | | | | | | | | | | |
| Picture 2 | | | | | | | | | | |
| Picture 3 | | | | | | | | | | |
| Picture 4 | | | | | | | | | | |
| Picture 5 | | | | | | | | | | |
| Brother | | | | | | | | | | |
| Cousin | | | | | | | | | | |
| Daughter | | | | | | | | | | |
| Mother | | | | | | | | | | |
| Uncle | | | | | | | | | | |

LEFT ⇦     RIGHT ⇨

1   2
3
4   5

| Picture | Subject | Relation |
|---|---|---|
| | | |
| | | |
| | | |
| | | |
| | | |

# Census

**62**

The town of Little Creek was recently the subject of a survey to assess the transport needs of its residents. To make administration easier, the town was divided into five regions, and a count was taken of the number of adults of working and non-working age in each area. Survey the clues below to discover the facts.

1 There are ninety fewer adults of non-working age than adults of working age in Region 4, and the number of adults of non-working age in Region 4 is higher than that in Region 3.

2 In one of the regions, there are 262 adults of working age and 282 adults of non-working age: higher in both cases than the number living in Region 1.

3 Region 2 has fewer adults of non-working age than Region 5.

4 Region 3 has fewer adults of working age than Region 5, but more adults of working age than Region 4.

|  | Working | | | | | Non-working | | | | |
|---|---|---|---|---|---|---|---|---|---|---|
|  | 220 | 231 | 240 | 262 | 282 | 131 | 141 | 150 | 282 | 300 |
| Region 1 |  |  |  |  |  |  |  |  |  |  |
| Region 2 |  |  |  |  |  |  |  |  |  |  |
| Region 3 |  |  |  |  |  |  |  |  |  |  |
| Region 4 |  |  |  |  |  |  |  |  |  |  |
| Region 5 |  |  |  |  |  |  |  |  |  |  |
| 131 |  |  |  |  |  |  |  |  |  |  |
| 141 |  |  |  |  |  |  |  |  |  |  |
| 150 |  |  |  |  |  |  |  |  |  |  |
| 282 |  |  |  |  |  |  |  |  |  |  |
| 300 |  |  |  |  |  |  |  |  |  |  |

| Region | Working | Non-working |
|---|---|---|
|  |  |  |
|  |  |  |
|  |  |  |
|  |  |  |
|  |  |  |

Non-working

# Playing Cards

The four men in this puzzle are playing a game of cards and each has three in his hand: one club, one diamond, and one spade. Can you discover which three cards are in each man's hand? (Note: A = ace, J=jack, Q=queen and K=king; and in the game, ace = 1, jack = 11, queen = 12, king = 13, and the values of the other cards are as per their numbers.)

**1** The value of the club held by the man with the ace of spades is lower than that of the club held by the man with the ten of diamonds.

**2** The man with the king of clubs has a spade with a value one lower than that of the diamond in Jimmy's hand. Jimmy's club has the same value as that of the spade he is holding.

**3** Liam's club has a lower value than that of his diamond which, in turn, has a lower value than that of his spade.

**4** Martin's diamond has a value one higher than that of his club.

|  | Club | | | | Diamond | | | | Spade | | | |
|---|---|---|---|---|---|---|---|---|---|---|---|---|
|  | A | 2 | 9 | K | 2 | 6 | 10 | Q | A | 6 | 9 | J |
| Jimmy |  |  |  |  |  |  |  |  |  |  |  |  |
| Keith |  |  |  |  |  |  |  |  |  |  |  |  |
| Liam |  |  |  |  |  |  |  |  |  |  |  |  |
| Martin |  |  |  |  |  |  |  |  |  |  |  |  |
| Spade A |  |  |  |  |  |  |  |  |  |  |  |  |
| Spade 6 |  |  |  |  |  |  |  |  |  |  |  |  |
| Spade 9 |  |  |  |  |  |  |  |  |  |  |  |  |
| Spade J |  |  |  |  |  |  |  |  |  |  |  |  |
| Diamond 2 |  |  |  |  |  |  |  |  |  |  |  |  |
| Diamond 6 |  |  |  |  |  |  |  |  |  |  |  |  |
| Diamond 10 |  |  |  |  |  |  |  |  |  |  |  |  |
| Diamond Q |  |  |  |  |  |  |  |  |  |  |  |  |

| Player | Club | Diamond | Spade |
|---|---|---|---|
|  |  |  |  |
|  |  |  |  |
|  |  |  |  |
|  |  |  |  |

# Visitors to London

When four youngsters visited their grandparents in England, each asked if they could be taken to London for the day, to see places of which they had heard. Their grandparents agreed and every child was taken to one place in the morning and a different place in the afternoon. On which day of the week did each child travel to London and which places did he or she visit?

1  The child who asked to visit Hyde Park also visited the Science Museum in the afternoon. His or her visit to London was the day after that of the child who enjoyed a ride on the London Eye.

2  Sarah climbed to the top of the Monument (built to commemorate the Great Fire of London in 1666) on Thursday, which was later in the week than Velma's trip to London.

3  The child who visited Buckingham Palace in the morning was taken to see the Globe Theatre in the afternoon.

4  Thomas (who didn't visit the Planetarium) visited London earlier than the child who went to Hyde Park.

|  | Day | | | | Morning | | | | Afternoon | | | |
|---|---|---|---|---|---|---|---|---|---|---|---|---|
|  | Tuesday | Wednesday | Thursday | Friday | B'ham Palace | Hyde Park | Planetarium | Tower of London | Globe Theatre | London Eye | Monument | Science Museum |
| Richard | | | | | | | | | | | | |
| Sarah | | | | | | | | | | | | |
| Thomas | | | | | | | | | | | | |
| Velma | | | | | | | | | | | | |
| Globe Theatre | | | | | | | | | | | | |
| London Eye | | | | | | | | | | | | |
| Monument | | | | | | | | | | | | |
| Science Mus | | | | | | | | | | | | |
| B'ham Palace | | | | | | | | | | | | |
| Hyde Park | | | | | | | | | | | | |
| Planetarium | | | | | | | | | | | | |
| T of London | | | | | | | | | | | | |

| Child | Day | Morning | Afternoon |
|---|---|---|---|
| | | | |
| | | | |
| | | | |
| | | | |

# Day Out

The children who appear in the previous puzzle were all taken out for the day during the second week of their visit, and one child (Thomas) had the good fortune to be taken out twice! Where did the children choose to go (in Thomas's case, there were two choices), and when was each outing?

1  The child taken to the art gallery isn't Velma, who went out the day before Richard.
2  Thomas's trip to the beach was later in the week than his visit to one of England's stately homes.
3  Velma isn't the child who visited a theme park on Monday.
4  No child was taken to see a castle on Friday.

|  | Visited | | | | | Day | | | | |
|---|---|---|---|---|---|---|---|---|---|---|
|  | Art gallery | Beach | Castle | Stately home | Theme park | Monday | Tuesday | Thursday | Friday | Saturday |
| Richard |  |  |  |  |  |  |  |  |  |  |
| Sarah |  |  |  |  |  |  |  |  |  |  |
| Thomas |  |  |  |  |  |  |  |  |  |  |
| Thomas |  |  |  |  |  |  |  |  |  |  |
| Velma |  |  |  |  |  |  |  |  |  |  |
| Monday |  |  |  |  |  |
| Tuesday |  |  |  |  |  |
| Thursday |  |  |  |  |  |
| Friday |  |  |  |  |  |
| Saturday |  |  |  |  |  |

| Child | Visited | Day |
|---|---|---|
|  |  |  |
|  |  |  |
|  |  |  |
|  |  |  |
|  |  |  |

# New Homes

The five couples in this puzzle all moved into new homes yesterday. Can you match each pair, and the number of the house they purchased?

(NB – As yet, No 5 has not been sold.)

1  Daphne lives directly south of Arthur.
2  Damian lives further east than Martin, who lives further north than Stephanie (who didn't move into the same house as Pete).
3  Penny lives further south than Lou, who lives further west than Steve.
4  Pete lives further east than Lou.

|  | Wife | | | | | House No | | | | |
|---|---|---|---|---|---|---|---|---|---|---|
|  | Daphne | Lou | Marie | Penny | Stephanie | 1 | 2 | 3 | 4 | 6 |
| Arthur |  |  |  |  |  |  |  |  |  |  |
| Damian |  |  |  |  |  |  |  |  |  |  |
| Martin |  |  |  |  |  |  |  |  |  |  |
| Pete |  |  |  |  |  |  |  |  |  |  |
| Steve |  |  |  |  |  |  |  |  |  |  |
| No 1 |  |  |  |  |  |
| No 2 |  |  |  |  |  |
| No 3 |  |  |  |  |  |
| No 4 |  |  |  |  |  |
| No 6 |  |  |  |  |  |

| Husband | Wife | House No |
|---|---|---|
|  |  |  |
|  |  |  |
|  |  |  |
|  |  |  |
|  |  |  |

# Party Time

Four children celebrated their birthdays last week, and each had a party on a different day to anyone else's, so all were able to attend one another's parties! What is each child's full name, on which day was his or her party, and how many guests were invited?

1 The child named McNeil had one fewer guest than Joanne, but more guests than six.

2 The child named Flinders had his or her party the day before that to which seven guests were invited, but the day after Brendan's party.

3 The child named Osgood held his or her party on Saturday afternoon.

4 A total of six children attended the party held on Wednesday afternoon.

5 Wayne's last name is neither Church nor McNeil. Brendan's last name isn't Church.

|  | Last name | | | | Day | | | | Guests | | | |
|---|---|---|---|---|---|---|---|---|---|---|---|---|
|  | Church | Flinders | McNeil | Osgood | Wednesday | Thursday | Friday | Saturday | 6 | 7 | 8 | 9 |
| Brendan | | | | | | | | | | | | |
| Joanne | | | | | | | | | | | | |
| Lara | | | | | | | | | | | | |
| Wayne | | | | | | | | | | | | |
| 6 guests | | | | | | | | | | | | |
| 7 guests | | | | | | | | | | | | |
| 8 guests | | | | | | | | | | | | |
| 9 guests | | | | | | | | | | | | |
| Wednesday | | | | | | | | | | | | |
| Thursday | | | | | | | | | | | | |
| Friday | | | | | | | | | | | | |
| Saturday | | | | | | | | | | | | |

| Child | Last name | Day | Guests |
|---|---|---|---|
| | | | |
| | | | |
| | | | |
| | | | |

# Astro-logical

Except for baby Billy, the four members of the Barnes family all read their horoscopes with great interest every day. What is the star sign and relationship to Billy of each member of the family, and what do their horoscopes predict for them today?

**1** The stars predicted that today would be a good day for love for the Piscean, who isn't Billy's father.

**2** Brenda's star sign is Aquarius, and Anita's prediction was that she would have a tough task to face today.

**3** Mark's star sign is Scorpio. His prediction wasn't that he would have a day that was good for money, nor did Billy's mother's horoscope predict that the day would be good for money.

| | Sign | | | | Relation | | | | Prediction | | | |
|---|---|---|---|---|---|---|---|---|---|---|---|---|
| | Aquarius | Aries | Pisces | Scorpio | Brother | Father | Mother | Sister | Good for love | Good for money | New friend | Tough task |
| Anita | | | | | | | | | | | | |
| Brenda | | | | | | | | | | | | |
| Mark | | | | | | | | | | | | |
| Micky | | | | | | | | | | | | |
| Good for love | | | | | | | | | | | | |
| Good for money | | | | | | | | | | | | |
| New friend | | | | | | | | | | | | |
| Tough task | | | | | | | | | | | | |
| Brother | | | | | | | | | | | | |
| Father | | | | | | | | | | | | |
| Mother | | | | | | | | | | | | |
| Sister | | | | | | | | | | | | |

| Name | Sign | Relation | Prediction |
|---|---|---|---|
| | | | |
| | | | |
| | | | |
| | | | |

# Split Personalities

Fed up with hearing too much about small-time celebrities, Sue has taken photographs of five of them, and cut each into three pieces (head, body and legs), and then reassembled them in such a way that each "new" picture contains pieces of three "old" ones. How have the pictures been reassembled?

1 Dave Day's body is in the same picture as Faye Fisher's legs.
2 Tommy Tow's legs are in the same picture as Mandy Miles's head, but not Faye Fisher's body.
3 Eddie Ego's head now tops the body of Mandy Miles.
4 Eddie Ego's legs are in a different picture to that of Tommy Tow's body.

| Head \ | Body: Dave Day | Eddie Ego | Faye Fisher | Mandy Miles | Tommy Tow | Legs: Dave Day | Eddie Ego | Faye Fisher | Mandy Miles | Tommy Tow |
|---|---|---|---|---|---|---|---|---|---|---|
| Dave Day | | | | | | | | | | |
| Eddie Ego | | | | | | | | | | |
| Faye Fisher | | | | | | | | | | |
| Mandy Miles | | | | | | | | | | |
| Tommy Tow | | | | | | | | | | |
| Legs: Dave Day | | | | | | | | | | |
| Eddie Ego | | | | | | | | | | |
| Faye Fisher | | | | | | | | | | |
| Mandy Miles | | | | | | | | | | |
| Tommy Tow | | | | | | | | | | |

| Head | Body | Legs |
|---|---|---|
| | | |
| | | |
| | | |
| | | |
| | | |

73

# Different Windows

Five residents of the block you see in the diagram below have all hung differently-shaded drapes in their windows. Can you discover who lives where and the details of his or her drapes?

1  The beige drapes are hanging in the window of an apartment on a different floor than Mrs Morgan's, and on a floor one higher than Mr Venner's.

2  Mr Pugh's drapes are a very dark blue. His apartment is directly next to and below that with beige drapes at the windows.

3  There are pale green drapes at the windows of No 3.

4  Mrs Quail lives in the apartment next to and left of that belonging to Miss Turk (which is not the one with yellow drapes at the windows).

|  | Resident | | | | | Curtains | | | | |
|---|---|---|---|---|---|---|---|---|---|---|
|  | Mrs Morgan | Mr Pugh | Mrs Quail | Miss Turk | Mr Venner | Beige | Blue | Cream | Green | Yellow |
| No 1 | | | | | | | | | | |
| No 2 | | | | | | | | | | |
| No 3 | | | | | | | | | | |
| No 4 | | | | | | | | | | |
| No 5 | | | | | | | | | | |
| Beige | | | | | | | | | | |
| Blue | | | | | | | | | | |
| Cream | | | | | | | | | | |
| Green | | | | | | | | | | |
| Yellow | | | | | | | | | | |

LEFT ⇦    RIGHT ⇨

| Apartment | Resident | Curtains |
|---|---|---|
| | | |
| | | |
| | | |
| | | |
| | | |

# Mid-Afternoon Break

Four people are seated at a table, as shown on the plan below. Each has a drink and a slice of cake. Can you discover the name of the occupant of each seat, together with what he or she chose to eat and drink?

1 Frank is seated clockwise of the person enjoying a slice of almond cake, who is seated clockwise of the person drinking cocoa.

2 The person drinking black coffee is seated clockwise of the person who has a slice of walnut cake, who is seated clockwise of Pauline.

3 The person who has a glass of milk (but who isn't in seat 4) is sitting clockwise of whoever has a slice of chocolate cake, who is sitting clockwise of Stella.

4 James has seat 1 on the plan below.

|  | Name | | | | Cake | | | | Drink | | | |
|---|---|---|---|---|---|---|---|---|---|---|---|---|
|  | Frank | James | Pauline | Stella | Almond | Chocolate | Fruit | Walnut | Black coffee | Cocoa | Milk | White coffee |
| Seat 1 |  |  |  |  |  |  |  |  |  |  |  |  |
| Seat 2 |  |  |  |  |  |  |  |  |  |  |  |  |
| Seat 3 |  |  |  |  |  |  |  |  |  |  |  |  |
| Seat 4 |  |  |  |  |  |  |  |  |  |  |  |  |
| Black coffee |  |  |  |  |  |  |  |  |
| Cocoa |  |  |  |  |  |  |  |  |
| Milk |  |  |  |  |  |  |  |  |
| White coffee |  |  |  |  |  |  |  |  |
| Almond |  |  |  |  |
| Chocolate |  |  |  |  |
| Fruit |  |  |  |  |
| Walnut |  |  |  |  |

**Clockwise**

1
4    2
3

| Seat | Name | Cake | Drink |
|---|---|---|---|
|  |  |  |  |
|  |  |  |  |
|  |  |  |  |
|  |  |  |  |

# Journeying Widely

**72**

Four businessmen each made trips to three different capital cities last month. No man visited more than one city on any date, and no man went to any city on precisely the same date as any of the others. On which dates was each city visited by every man?

1 The man who visited Madrid on the 11th went to Vienna four days before he went to Ottawa.

2 The man who went to Ottawa on the 11th was in Vienna on the day that Will was in Madrid.

3 The man who was in Ottawa on the 17th was in Vienna earlier in the month than Brian.

4 Dennis visited Madrid later in the month than he went to Vienna.

5 Jamie's trip to Ottawa was earlier in the month than he visited Madrid.

|  | Madrid | | | | Ottawa | | | | Vienna | | | |
|---|---|---|---|---|---|---|---|---|---|---|---|---|
|  | 4th | 8th | 11th | 15th | 8th | 11th | 17th | 19th | 4th | 11th | 15th | 19th |
| Brian | | | | | | | | | | | | |
| Dennis | | | | | | | | | | | | |
| Jamie | | | | | | | | | | | | |
| Will | | | | | | | | | | | | |
| Vienna 4th | | | | | | | | | | | | |
| Vienna 11th | | | | | | | | | | | | |
| Vienna 15th | | | | | | | | | | | | |
| Vienna 19th | | | | | | | | | | | | |
| Ottawa 8th | | | | | | | | | | | | |
| Ottawa 11th | | | | | | | | | | | | |
| Ottawa 17th | | | | | | | | | | | | |
| Ottawa 19th | | | | | | | | | | | | |

| Name | Madrid | Ottawa | Vienna |
|---|---|---|---|
|  |  |  |  |
|  |  |  |  |
|  |  |  |  |
|  |  |  |  |

76

# Going to Work

The people occupying the seats shown in the train carriage below are all commuters, on their way to work. Can you discover who has each seat, as well as his or her job? (NB – Seat 4 is empty.)

1  The engineer isn't sitting directly next to the empty seat.

2  Mr Grover (who works as a psychologist) has a seat with a number higher than that of the secretary, who is neither Miss Blake nor Mr Harte.

3  Mrs Young has the highest numbered seat in the carriage.

4  Mrs Neville is sitting directly next to the clerk and directly opposite Mr Harte.

|  | Name | | | | | Job | | | | |
|---|---|---|---|---|---|---|---|---|---|---|
|  | Miss Blake | Mr Grover | Mr Harte | Mrs Neville | Mrs Young | Analyst | Clerk | Engineer | Psychologist | Secretary |
| Seat 1 |  |  |  |  |  |  |  |  |  |  |
| Seat 2 |  |  |  |  |  |  |  |  |  |  |
| Seat 3 |  |  |  |  |  |  |  |  |  |  |
| Seat 5 |  |  |  |  |  |  |  |  |  |  |
| Seat 6 |  |  |  |  |  |  |  |  |  |  |
| Analyst |  |  |  |  |  |
| Clerk |  |  |  |  |  |
| Engineer |  |  |  |  |  |
| Psychologist |  |  |  |  |  |
| Secretary |  |  |  |  |  |

| 1 | 2 | 3 |
|---|---|---|
|  |  |  |
| 4 | 5 | 6 |

| Seat | Name | Job |
|---|---|---|
|  |  |  |
|  |  |  |
|  |  |  |
|  |  |  |
|  |  |  |

# Fruit Farmers

Five Spanish fruit growers and their families each specialize in growing a particular kind of fruit. Can you match each farm on the map below to the type of fruit grown, and the number of years the family has been resident there?

1 The melons aren't growing at farm E.

2 The owners of farm E have been there for nine years longer than the family that owns the vineyard, which produces dessert grapes for export.

3 The farm at which figs are grown is directly west of that which has been occupied by the same family for 33 years.

4 The family that has been in residence for the shortest period of time have an orange-producing farm.

5 The family that grows lemons have occupied their farm for nine years longer than the people who live at farm A.

|  | Fruit | | | | | Years | | | | |
|---|---|---|---|---|---|---|---|---|---|---|
|  | Figs | Grapes | Lemons | Melons | Oranges | 15 | 18 | 24 | 27 | 33 |
| Farm A |  |  |  |  |  |  |  |  |  |  |
| Farm B |  |  |  |  |  |  |  |  |  |  |
| Farm C |  |  |  |  |  |  |  |  |  |  |
| Farm D |  |  |  |  |  |  |  |  |  |  |
| Farm E |  |  |  |  |  |  |  |  |  |  |
| 15 years |  |  |  |  |  | | | | | |
| 18 years |  |  |  |  |  | | | | | |
| 24 years |  |  |  |  |  | | | | | |
| 27 years |  |  |  |  |  | | | | | |
| 33 years |  |  |  |  |  | | | | | |

N
W E
S

A    B

C    D

E

| Farm | Fruit | Years |
|---|---|---|
|  |  |  |
|  |  |  |
|  |  |  |
|  |  |  |
|  |  |  |

# Getting to Work

Four employees at the NBC bank each take a different length of time to get to work every morning. Can you identify each employee by his or her full name, job in the bank, and journey time?

1 The employee named Masters takes 14 minutes to get to work, which is less time than it takes Larry.

2 The chief cashier takes 18 minutes to get to work, which is longer than it takes the employee named Wilson.

3 Maggie Poulter takes four minutes longer to get to work than the manager of the NBC bank.

4 The security guard takes less time to get to work than Pippa.

|  | Last name | | | | Position | | | | Time (mins) | | | |
|---|---|---|---|---|---|---|---|---|---|---|---|---|
|  | Cooke | Masters | Poulter | Wilson | Asst Manager | Chief Cashier | Manager | Security Guard | 10 | 14 | 18 | 22 |
| Larry |  |  |  |  |  |  |  |  |  |  |  |  |
| Maggie |  |  |  |  |  |  |  |  |  |  |  |  |
| Pippa |  |  |  |  |  |  |  |  |  |  |  |  |
| Warren |  |  |  |  |  |  |  |  |  |  |  |  |
| 10 minutes |  |  |  |  |  |  |  |  | | | | |
| 14 minutes |  |  |  |  |  |  |  |  | | | | |
| 18 minutes |  |  |  |  |  |  |  |  | | | | |
| 22 minutes |  |  |  |  |  |  |  |  | | | | |
| Asst Manager |  |  |  |  | | | | | | | | |
| Chief Cashier |  |  |  |  | | | | | | | | |
| Manager |  |  |  |  | | | | | | | | |
| Security Guard |  |  |  |  | | | | | | | | |

| Employee | Last name | Position | Time |
|---|---|---|---|
|  |  |  |  |
|  |  |  |  |
|  |  |  |  |
|  |  |  |  |

# Out of the Race

At a fund-raising car rally, four dilapidated vehicles were pulled out of the race at various stages. Use the clues below to discover the design painted onto each driver's vehicle, the number of pit stops it had to make, and the number of laps it completed before the officials decided it was no longer safe to compete.

1 The car with bright orange flames painted along each side made one fewer pit stop and completed one more lap than Michelle's vehicle.

2 The car painted entirely with a black and white checker design made one fewer pit stop and covered two more laps than Larry's car.

3 Clive's car was painted with a design of stripes in various shades of blue. It made one fewer pit stop than the car with the checker design.

4 Pat's dilapidated car made more than three pit stops.

| | Design | | | | Pit stops | | | | Laps | | | |
|---|---|---|---|---|---|---|---|---|---|---|---|---|
| | Blue stripes | Checkers | Flames | Fork lightning | 3 | 4 | 5 | 6 | 12 | 13 | 14 | 15 |
| Clive | | | | | | | | | | | | |
| Larry | | | | | | | | | | | | |
| Michelle | | | | | | | | | | | | |
| Pat | | | | | | | | | | | | |
| 12 laps | | | | | | | | | | | | |
| 13 laps | | | | | | | | | | | | |
| 14 laps | | | | | | | | | | | | |
| 15 laps | | | | | | | | | | | | |
| 3 pit stops | | | | | | | | | | | | |
| 4 pit stops | | | | | | | | | | | | |
| 5 pit stops | | | | | | | | | | | | |
| 6 pit stops | | | | | | | | | | | | |

| Driver | Design | Pit stops | Laps |
|---|---|---|---|
| | | | |
| | | | |
| | | | |
| | | | |

# Carpet Sales

Carl had five customers at his shop this morning, all of whom bought a bedroom carpet. At what time did each come into the shop, and what did he or she choose?

1. The person who chose the pink bedroom carpet came in one hour later than Mr Adams, who came in thirty minutes later than Miss Lawson.
2. The first customer of the day chose a dark green carpet.
3. Mrs Pitt came into the shop half an hour later than Miss Stone, who chose a carpet in a deep turquoise shade.
4. Mrs Cole wasn't Carl's fifth customer of the morning.
5. The lilac carpet wasn't Carl's third sale of the morning.

|  | Time | | | | | Carpet | | | | |
|---|---|---|---|---|---|---|---|---|---|---|
|  | 9.30am | 10.00am | 10.30am | 11.00am | 11.30am | Blue | Green | Lilac | Pink | Turquoise |
| Mr Adams |  |  |  |  |  |  |  |  |  |  |
| Mrs Cole |  |  |  |  |  |  |  |  |  |  |
| Miss Lawson |  |  |  |  |  |  |  |  |  |  |
| Mrs Pitt |  |  |  |  |  |  |  |  |  |  |
| Miss Stone |  |  |  |  |  |  |  |  |  |  |
| Blue |  |  |  |  |  |
| Green |  |  |  |  |  |
| Lilac |  |  |  |  |  |
| Pink |  |  |  |  |  |
| Turquoise |  |  |  |  |  |

| Customer | Time | Carpet |
|---|---|---|
|  |  |  |
|  |  |  |
|  |  |  |
|  |  |  |
|  |  |  |

# Parking Lot

The owners of the five cars parked in the lot as seen mapped below all travel various numbers of miles to work each day. Can you discover the owner of each vehicle, and the distance he or she travels to work?

1 On the map below, Gemima's car has a higher number than that driven by whoever covers three more miles than Gemima.

2 Alan travels three more miles than the owner of car number 5.

3 Hazel drives car number 3.

4 The woman who travels 22 miles to work each day drives a car that is parked directly north of Jeremy's.

5 Tricia drives further to work each day than the distance covered by Jeremy.

| | Driver | | | | | Distance (miles) | | | | |
|---|---|---|---|---|---|---|---|---|---|---|
| | Alan | Gemima | Hazel | Jeremy | Tricia | 14 | 17 | 19 | 22 | 25 |
| Car 1 | | | | | | | | | | |
| Car 2 | | | | | | | | | | |
| Car 3 | | | | | | | | | | |
| Car 4 | | | | | | | | | | |
| Car 5 | | | | | | | | | | |
| 14 miles | | | | | | | | | | |
| 17 miles | | | | | | | | | | |
| 19 miles | | | | | | | | | | |
| 22 miles | | | | | | | | | | |
| 25 miles | | | | | | | | | | |

N
W E
S

1 2

3 4 5

| Car | Driver | Distance |
|---|---|---|
| | | |
| | | |
| | | |
| | | |
| | | |

# The Electric Eighties

In the 1980s, James worked as an electrician for four popular bands who appeared in various resorts during the summer season. Can you work out where he was in each of the listed years, together with the name of the band, and its lead singer?

1 Debbie Dean was lead singer with Loose Ends, with whom James worked two seasons before he went to Deep Falls with one of the bands.

2 Fathers' Fear appeared one season at the Rocky Lake resort. This was in a later year than James worked as an electrician in Smallwood, but an earlier year than he worked with the band in which Phil Potter was lead singer.

3 Kathy Krush was lead singer of the band (not the Dormice) that performed at Ocean River, but not in 1986.

|  | Resort | | | | Band | | | | Singer | | | |
|---|---|---|---|---|---|---|---|---|---|---|---|---|
|  | Deep Falls | Ocean River | Rocky Lake | Smallwood | The Dormice | Fathers' Fear | Loose Ends | The Rave | Debbie Dean | Graeme Good | Kathy Krush | Phil Potter |
| 1983 | | | | | | | | | | | | |
| 1984 | | | | | | | | | | | | |
| 1985 | | | | | | | | | | | | |
| 1986 | | | | | | | | | | | | |
| Debbie Dean | | | | | | | | | | | | |
| Graeme Good | | | | | | | | | | | | |
| Kathy Krush | | | | | | | | | | | | |
| Phil Potter | | | | | | | | | | | | |
| The Dormice | | | | | | | | | | | | |
| Fathers' Fear | | | | | | | | | | | | |
| Loose Ends | | | | | | | | | | | | |
| The Rave | | | | | | | | | | | | |

|  |  |  |  |
|---|---|---|---|
|  |  |  |  |
|  |  |  |  |
|  |  |  |  |
|  |  |  |  |

# Room Service

It is almost midnight, but the night porter (who also provides room service) at the Parkside Hotel has just received requests for a drink and snack to be delivered to the guests in each of the four rooms on the fourth floor. Who is in each room, and what has he or she requested to eat and drink?

1 The guest who has ordered the blueberry muffin isn't in room 401. The guest who has requested a glass of orange juice isn't in room 404.

2 The guest who has ordered a glass of beer is in a room with a number one higher than that of the person who has asked for a club sandwich to be brought to the room.

3 Ms Moore (who has ordered a salad) is in a room with a higher number than that of Mr Fischer, to whom the whiskey and soda will be taken.

4 The guest who has ordered both a hamburger and coffee is in a room with a number one lower than that of Mrs Thorn.

|  | Guest | | | | Drink | | | | Food | | | |
|---|---|---|---|---|---|---|---|---|---|---|---|---|
|  | Mr Fischer | Ms Moore | Mrs Thorn | Mr Watson | Beer | Coffee | Orange juice | Whiskey/soda | Club sandwich | Hamburger | Muffin | Salad |
| Room 401 |  |  |  |  |  |  |  |  |  |  |  |  |
| Room 402 |  |  |  |  |  |  |  |  |  |  |  |  |
| Room 403 |  |  |  |  |  |  |  |  |  |  |  |  |
| Room 404 |  |  |  |  |  |  |  |  |  |  |  |  |
| Club sandwich |  |  |  |  |  |  |  |  |  |  |  |  |
| Hamburger |  |  |  |  |  |  |  |  |  |  |  |  |
| Muffin |  |  |  |  |  |  |  |  |  |  |  |  |
| Salad |  |  |  |  |  |  |  |  |  |  |  |  |
| Beer |  |  |  |  |  |  |  |  |  |  |  |  |
| Coffee |  |  |  |  |  |  |  |  |  |  |  |  |
| Orange juice |  |  |  |  |  |  |  |  |  |  |  |  |
| Whiskey/soda |  |  |  |  |  |  |  |  |  |  |  |  |

| Room | Guest | Drink | Food |
|---|---|---|---|
|  |  |  |  |
|  |  |  |  |
|  |  |  |  |
|  |  |  |  |

# Maternity Muddle

Five couples are celebrating the arrival of their first
child – each born yesterday at the local hospital. Can
you match each couple together with their baby?

1 Roy isn't Sally's husband or Philip's father. Nor is Philip's father
Peter.
2 Peter's baby isn't Joy and Joy's father isn't Mike.
3 Mary gave birth to May, who is heavier than Peter's child.
4 Sammy's mother isn't Pamela.
5 Sonja is married to Mike. Sally isn't the mother of Peter's baby.
6 Ray isn't the father of Philip, whose mother is Rachel.

|  | Mother | | | | | Baby | | | | |
|---|---|---|---|---|---|---|---|---|---|---|
|  | Mary | Pamela | Rachel | Sally | Sonja | Dennis | Joy | May | Philip | Sammy |
| Mike |  |  |  |  |  |  |  |  |  |  |
| Peter |  |  |  |  |  |  |  |  |  |  |
| Ray |  |  |  |  |  |  |  |  |  |  |
| Roy |  |  |  |  |  |  |  |  |  |  |
| Steve |  |  |  |  |  |  |  |  |  |  |
| Dennis |  |  |  |  |  |  |
| Joy |  |  |  |  |  |  |
| May |  |  |  |  |  |  |
| Philip |  |  |  |  |  |  |
| Sammy |  |  |  |  |  |  |

| Father | Mother | Baby |
|---|---|---|
|  |  |  |
|  |  |  |
|  |  |  |
|  |  |  |
|  |  |  |

# Party Girls

Five girls of different ages are having parties today, as each is celebrating her birthday. Every girl lives in a different house (as shown on the plan below). Can you work through the clues to discover not only where each girl lives, but also her age today?

**1** Pamela and Tracey are both younger than the girl who lives at No 7.

**2** Bella and Pamela both live further east than the girl who is celebrating her tenth birthday today.

**3** The twelve-year-old lives neither furthest east nor furthest west.

**4** Colette and Tracey both live further east than Nadine, who isn't celebrating her eleventh birthday.

**5** The girl at No 9 isn't Bella. Neither the nine-year-old girl nor the eleven-year-old girl lives at No 9.

**6** The girl who is nine years old lives further east than Tracey.

|  | Girl | | | | | Age | | | | |
|---|---|---|---|---|---|---|---|---|---|---|
|  | Bella | Colette | Nadine | Pamela | Tracey | 9 | 10 | 11 | 12 | 13 |
| No 1 | | | | | | | | | | |
| No 3 | | | | | | | | | | |
| No 5 | | | | | | | | | | |
| No 7 | | | | | | | | | | |
| No 9 | | | | | | | | | | |
| 9 years old | | | | | | | | | | |
| 10 years old | | | | | | | | | | |
| 11 years old | | | | | | | | | | |
| 12 years old | | | | | | | | | | |
| 13 years old | | | | | | | | | | |

N
W — E
S

| 1 | 3 | 5 | 7 | 9 |

| House No | Girl | Age |
|---|---|---|
| | | |
| | | |
| | | |
| | | |
| | | |

# Celebrity Interviews

Journalist Ivor Pencill covers celebrity interviews for the popular magazine *Starstruck*. Last week he was lucky enough to secure some time with four different women, all major stars. Can you discover the town to which he journeyed to meet each woman on the listed days, together with her name and occupation?

1 Ivor went to Appleton the day after he interviewed the television producer, but the day before his meeting with Mary Kay (which didn't take place in Oakfield).

2 Anni Jones is an actress strongly tipped for an Oscar next year. Ivor's interview with her took place the day before he journeyed to Oakfield.

3 Westford was the location of Ivor's meeting with the rock singer, who was interviewed by him the day after he spoke to Naomi Noon.

|  | Town | | | | Celebrity | | | | Occupation | | | |
|---|---|---|---|---|---|---|---|---|---|---|---|---|
|  | Appleton | Dayville | Oakfield | Westford | Anni Jones | Mary Kay | Naomi Noon | Suzi Taylor | Actress | Dancer | Singer | TV producer |
| Tuesday |  |  |  |  |  |  |  |  |  |  |  |  |
| Wednesday |  |  |  |  |  |  |  |  |  |  |  |  |
| Thursday |  |  |  |  |  |  |  |  |  |  |  |  |
| Friday |  |  |  |  |  |  |  |  |  |  |  |  |
| Actress |  |  |  |  |  |  |  |  |  |  |  |  |
| Dancer |  |  |  |  |  |  |  |  |  |  |  |  |
| Singer |  |  |  |  |  |  |  |  |  |  |  |  |
| TV producer |  |  |  |  |  |  |  |  |  |  |  |  |
| Anni Jones |  |  |  |  |  |  |  |  |  |  |  |  |
| Mary Kay |  |  |  |  |  |  |  |  |  |  |  |  |
| Naomi Noon |  |  |  |  |  |  |  |  |  |  |  |  |
| Suzi Taylor |  |  |  |  |  |  |  |  |  |  |  |  |

| Day | Town | Celebrity | Occupation |
|---|---|---|---|
|  |  |  |  |
|  |  |  |  |
|  |  |  |  |
|  |  |  |  |

# Plane Mistakes

Four members of the Ditchmore Gliding Club got into difficulties last week, and were forced to land their planes in places where they really shouldn't have been! Which glider does each man own, on which day did his problem occur, and where did he land?

1  It was on Friday that Des lost his bearings and landed on the army firing range at Ditchmore – scaring the soldiers almost as much as they and their rifles scared him!

2  The pilot of the blue glider made his mistake earlier in the week than the man who put down his plane among the zebra in the nearby safari park.

3  Jim has a yellow glider. The white glider's pilot was fortunate to find a break in the traffic large enough to enable him to land on the main road to Ditchmore.

4  Colin's mistake was made the day before that of the pilot of the purple glider.

|  | Glider | | | | Day | | | | Landed | | | |
|---|---|---|---|---|---|---|---|---|---|---|---|---|
|  | Blue | Purple | White | Yellow | Monday | Tuesday | Thursday | Friday | Beach | Firing range | Main road | Safari park |
| Aidan | | | | | | | | | | | | |
| Colin | | | | | | | | | | | | |
| Des | | | | | | | | | | | | |
| Jim | | | | | | | | | | | | |
| Beach | | | | | | | | | |
| Firing range | | | | | | | | | |
| Main road | | | | | | | | | |
| Safari park | | | | | | | | | |
| Monday | | | | | |
| Tuesday | | | | | |
| Thursday | | | | | |
| Friday | | | | | |

| Pilot | Glider | Day | Landed |
|---|---|---|---|
|  |  |  |  |
|  |  |  |  |
|  |  |  |  |
|  |  |  |  |

# Viewing Habits

Five friends who share a house each have one television show which he or she insists on watching every week. Which show does each friend watch, and on which evening of the week?

1 Laurence's show is broadcast two nights before *Cartoon Capers*, which Jessica would never miss!

2 On Tuesday evenings, one of the men insists on watching *Laugh a Lot* which, as you may have guessed, is a comedy show.

3 Simon's preference is for *News Review*, which is broadcast the evening before *World's End*, a popular soap opera.

4 *Sports Slot* is broadcast on Monday evenings.

|  | Cartoon Capers | Laugh a Lot | News Review | Sports Slot | World's End | Monday | Tuesday | Thursday | Friday | Sunday |
|---|---|---|---|---|---|---|---|---|---|---|
| Alan |  |  |  |  |  |  |  |  |  |  |
| Jessica |  |  |  |  |  |  |  |  |  |  |
| Karen |  |  |  |  |  |  |  |  |  |  |
| Laurence |  |  |  |  |  |  |  |  |  |  |
| Simon |  |  |  |  |  |  |  |  |  |  |
| Monday |  |  |  |  |  |  |  |  |  |  |
| Tuesday |  |  |  |  |  |  |  |  |  |  |
| Thursday |  |  |  |  |  |  |  |  |  |  |
| Friday |  |  |  |  |  |  |  |  |  |  |
| Sunday |  |  |  |  |  |  |  |  |  |  |

| Viewer | Show | Evening |
|---|---|---|
|  |  |  |
|  |  |  |
|  |  |  |
|  |  |  |
|  |  |  |

# Visitors

Five of the elderly folk who live in Church View received visits from their relatives last week. Can you discover who lives in each of the residences shown on the map below, and find out the identity of each person's visitor?

1 The resident whose son paid a visit lives in a house with a number two higher than that which is home to Thomas.

2 Louise's house has a number one higher than that of the person who received a visit from his or her daughter.

3 No 8 Church View is home to John.

4 Brenda (who doesn't live at No 12) received a visit from her eldest grandson.

5 Sarah lives directly north of the resident whose niece came to call.

|  | Resident | | | | | Visitor | | | | |
|---|---|---|---|---|---|---|---|---|---|---|
|  | Brenda | John | Louise | Sarah | Thomas | Daughter | Grandson | Nephew | Niece | Son |
| No 6 |  |  |  |  |  |  |  |  |  |  |
| No 8 |  |  |  |  |  |  |  |  |  |  |
| No 9 |  |  |  |  |  |  |  |  |  |  |
| No 10 |  |  |  |  |  |  |  |  |  |  |
| No 12 |  |  |  |  |  |  |  |  |  |  |
| Daughter |  |  |  |  |  |
| Grandson |  |  |  |  |  |
| Nephew |  |  |  |  |  |
| Niece |  |  |  |  |  |
| Son |  |  |  |  |  |

| House No | Resident | Visitor |
|---|---|---|
|  |  |  |
|  |  |  |
|  |  |  |
|  |  |  |
|  |  |  |

# Sick Days

Ed Ayke didn't tell his mother that he was due to take end of year exams on different days over the course of four weeks: instead, he decided to feign illness on those days – a fact which only became known to his mother when she attended the annual Parents' Evening! For each of the four weeks, discover the day on which the examination took place, the subject it covered, and the excuse Ed Ayke gave to his mother which prompted her to keep him off school.

1 Instead of taking his English test, Ed gave his mother a testing time by complaining of dizzy spells, and occasionally swaying back and forth in an alarming way.

2 A throbbing pain deep within his ear was an excuse that sounded convincing to Mrs Ayke one Tuesday morning. This excuse was given the week before Ed should have taken a geography examination.

3 Monday's mathematics test was avoided in week 3, but wasn't the examination Ed avoided by falling on the floor and saying he couldn't walk because of an injury to his knee.

4 The examination in week 4 wasn't on a Thursday.

|  | Day | | | | Subject | | | | Excuse | | | |
|---|---|---|---|---|---|---|---|---|---|---|---|---|
|  | Monday | Tuesday | Wednesday | Thursday | English | Geography | Mathematics | Science | Dizzy spells | Earache | Knee injury | Stomach pains |
| Week 1 |  |  |  |  |  |  |  |  |  |  |  |  |
| Week 2 |  |  |  |  |  |  |  |  |  |  |  |  |
| Week 3 |  |  |  |  |  |  |  |  |  |  |  |  |
| Week 4 |  |  |  |  |  |  |  |  |  |  |  |  |
| Dizzy spells |  |  |  |  |  |  |  |  |  |  |  |  |
| Earache |  |  |  |  |  |  |  |  |  |  |  |  |
| Knee injury |  |  |  |  |  |  |  |  |  |  |  |  |
| Stomach pains |  |  |  |  |  |  |  |  |  |  |  |  |
| English |  |  |  |  |  |  |  |  |  |  |  |  |
| Geography |  |  |  |  |  |  |  |  |  |  |  |  |
| Mathematics |  |  |  |  |  |  |  |  |  |  |  |  |
| Science |  |  |  |  |  |  |  |  |  |  |  |  |

| Week | Day | Subject | Excuse |
|---|---|---|---|
|  |  |  |  |
|  |  |  |  |
|  |  |  |  |
|  |  |  |  |

# Facing the Music

The diagram below was drawn from a position behind the musicians, so their view of "left" and "right" is the same as yours as you look at the picture. Can you match each performer to his or her position on the diagram, the instrument he or she plays, and his or her age?

1 The oldest of the four musicians doesn't play the tuba. Patricia is not the youngest player.

2 The cello player is more than one year younger than the musician directly next to and left of him/her.

3 The violinist is further right than (but not directly next to) Leanne, who is either two years older or two years younger than the violinist.

4 Tom is three years older than the flute player, who isn't Patricia.

|  | Position | | | | Instrument | | | | Age | | | |
|---|---|---|---|---|---|---|---|---|---|---|---|---|
|  | A | B | C | D | Cello | Flute | Violin | Tuba | 38 | 41 | 42 | 44 |
| Charles |  |  |  |  |  |  |  |  |  |  |  |  |
| Leanne |  |  |  |  |  |  |  |  |  |  |  |  |
| Patricia |  |  |  |  |  |  |  |  |  |  |  |  |
| Tom |  |  |  |  |  |  |  |  |  |  |  |  |
| 38 years old |  |  |  |  |  |  |  |  |  |  |  |  |
| 41 years old |  |  |  |  |  |  |  |  |  |  |  |  |
| 42 years old |  |  |  |  |  |  |  |  |  |  |  |  |
| 44 years old |  |  |  |  |  |  |  |  |  |  |  |  |
| Cello |  |  |  |  |  |  |  |  |  |  |  |  |
| Flute |  |  |  |  |  |  |  |  |  |  |  |  |
| Violin |  |  |  |  |  |  |  |  |  |  |  |  |
| Tuba |  |  |  |  |  |  |  |  |  |  |  |  |

LEFT ⇦          RIGHT ⇨

A    B    C    D

| Musician | Position | Instrument | Age |
|---|---|---|---|
|  |  |  |  |
|  |  |  |  |
|  |  |  |  |
|  |  |  |  |

# Get Set

All five of the Racket sisters played tennis last Saturday afternoon, and each managed to play two sets before rain forced everyone to abandon the event. How many games did each of the Racket sisters win against their individual opponents?

1. Cora won half as many games in the second set as she had won in the first set.
2. Flora won two fewer games than Nora in the second set.
3. Laura won three fewer games in the second set as she had won in the first set.
4. No-one won the same total number of games as anyone else.

|  | 1st Set | | | | | 2nd Set | | | | |
|---|---|---|---|---|---|---|---|---|---|---|
|  | 3 | 4 | 5 | 6 | 7 | 3 | 4 | 5 | 6 | 7 |
| Cora |  |  |  |  |  |  |  |  |  |  |
| Dora |  |  |  |  |  |  |  |  |  |  |
| Flora |  |  |  |  |  |  |  |  |  |  |
| Laura |  |  |  |  |  |  |  |  |  |  |
| Nora |  |  |  |  |  |  |  |  |  |  |
| 2nd Set 3 |  |  |  |  |  |
| 4 |  |  |  |  |  |
| 5 |  |  |  |  |  |
| 6 |  |  |  |  |  |
| 7 |  |  |  |  |  |

| Player | 1st Set | 2nd Set |
|---|---|---|
|  |  |  |
|  |  |  |
|  |  |  |
|  |  |  |
|  |  |  |

# Easter Eggs

Last Easter, Evelyn bought an Easter egg each for her daughters, plus one for herself of course! This puzzle, however, concerns only those eggs for the daughters … Can you discover the order in which Evelyn bought each girl's egg, together with details of the foil in which it was wrapped?

1 The egg wrapped in orange foil was bought immediately after Deborah's, which was bought later than the egg wrapped in silver foil, which wasn't purchased first.

2 The egg bought by Evelyn for Samantha was purchased earlier than that wrapped in pink foil, which wasn't given to Deborah.

3 The egg given to Jasmine was bought immediately before the egg wrapped in gold foil, but later than the egg purchased for Belinda.

4 Jessica's egg wasn't wrapped in orange foil.

|  | Order | | | | | Foil | | | | |
|---|---|---|---|---|---|---|---|---|---|---|
|  | First | Second | Third | Fourth | Fifth | Gold | Orange | Pink | Purple | Silver |
| Belinda |  |  |  |  |  |  |  |  |  |  |
| Deborah |  |  |  |  |  |  |  |  |  |  |
| Jasmine |  |  |  |  |  |  |  |  |  |  |
| Jessica |  |  |  |  |  |  |  |  |  |  |
| Samantha |  |  |  |  |  |  |  |  |  |  |
| Gold |  |  |  |  |  |
| Orange |  |  |  |  |  |
| Pink |  |  |  |  |  |
| Purple |  |  |  |  |  |
| Silver |  |  |  |  |  |

| Daughter | Order | Foil |
|---|---|---|
|  |  |  |
|  |  |  |
|  |  |  |
|  |  |  |
|  |  |  |

# A Good Match

Four members of a modelmaking club have painstakingly assembled matchstick models as gifts for relatives. Which model has each person made, how many matchsticks were used in its construction, and to which relative will it be presented?

1 The man who lovingly constructed a miniature replica of the Taj Mahal as a gift for his wife on their eighteenth wedding anniversary used more matchsticks than Jane.

2 Whoever used the most matchsticks intends his model as a gift for his uncle's birthday next month. This model isn't of London's Tower Bridge.

3 Cliff used fewer than 4,344 matches to make his model, which isn't for his wife or brother.

4 Someone's brother will receive the carefully crafted model of Toronto's CN Tower, which wasn't made with the 2,468 matchsticks.

5 Paul's model isn't of the Eiffel Tower in Paris.

|  | Model | | | | Matches | | | | For | | | |
|---|---|---|---|---|---|---|---|---|---|---|---|---|
|  | CN Tower | Eiffel Tower | Tower Bridge | Taj Mahal | 2,468 | 3,715 | 4,022 | 4,344 | Brother | Nephew | Uncle | Wife |
| Cliff |  |  |  |  |  |  |  |  |  |  |  |  |
| Jane |  |  |  |  |  |  |  |  |  |  |  |  |
| Paul |  |  |  |  |  |  |  |  |  |  |  |  |
| Ron |  |  |  |  |  |  |  |  |  |  |  |  |
| Brother |  |  |  |  |  |  |  |  |  |  |  |  |
| Nephew |  |  |  |  |  |  |  |  |  |  |  |  |
| Uncle |  |  |  |  |  |  |  |  |  |  |  |  |
| Wife |  |  |  |  |  |  |  |  |  |  |  |  |
| 2,468 |  |  |  |  |  |  |  |  |  |  |  |  |
| 3,715 |  |  |  |  |  |  |  |  |  |  |  |  |
| 4,022 |  |  |  |  |  |  |  |  |  |  |  |  |
| 4,344 |  |  |  |  |  |  |  |  |  |  |  |  |

| Maker | Model | Matches | For |
|---|---|---|---|
|  |  |  |  |
|  |  |  |  |
|  |  |  |  |
|  |  |  |  |

# Shopping Trips

Each of the four women in this puzzle visited three different shops this morning and no woman visited the same shop in the same order as anyone else. Can you discover the order in which they shopped?

1 The woman who went to the butcher first went third to the shop visited first by Diane, who went to the newsagent third.

2 Mandy went first to the shop which Diane visited second.

3 Sue went to the grocer first.

|  | First | | | | Second | | | | Third | | | |
|---|---|---|---|---|---|---|---|---|---|---|---|---|
|  | Baker | Butcher | Grocer | Newsagent | Baker | Butcher | Grocer | Newsagent | Baker | Butcher | Grocer | Newsagent |
| Cheryl | | | | | | | | | | | | |
| Diane | | | | | | | | | | | | |
| Mandy | | | | | | | | | | | | |
| Sue | | | | | | | | | | | | |
| Third Baker | | | | | | | | | | | | |
| Third Butcher | | | | | | | | | | | | |
| Third Grocer | | | | | | | | | | | | |
| Third Newsagent | | | | | | | | | | | | |
| Second Baker | | | | | | | | | | | | |
| Second Butcher | | | | | | | | | | | | |
| Second Grocer | | | | | | | | | | | | |
| Second Newsagent | | | | | | | | | | | | |

| Shopper | First | Second | Third |
|---|---|---|---|
| | | | |
| | | | |
| | | | |
| | | | |

# Cat Conundrum

Five cats and their owners live in various houses in Kittyville. Can you discover the feline facts? The clues and map below should help.

1 Daisy and Cuthbert live together in a house with a higher number than Colin's.

2 Chris lives further west than Nero and his owner, and further north than Sooty and his owner.

3 Caitlin lives in the house with a number three lower than that which is home to Marmaduke and his owner.

4 Cathy and her cat don't live directly north of Cuthbert.

|  | \multicolumn{5}{c}{Cat} | \multicolumn{5}{c}{Owner} |
|---|---|---|---|---|---|---|---|---|---|---|
|  | Daisy | Lucky | Marmaduke | Nero | Sooty | Caitlin | Cathy | Chris | Colin | Cuthbert |
| No 1 |  |  |  |  |  |  |  |  |  |  |
| No 2 |  |  |  |  |  |  |  |  |  |  |
| No 3 |  |  |  |  |  |  |  |  |  |  |
| No 4 |  |  |  |  |  |  |  |  |  |  |
| No 5 |  |  |  |  |  |  |  |  |  |  |
| Caitlin |  |  |  |  |  |
| Cathy |  |  |  |  |  |
| Chris |  |  |  |  |  |
| Colin |  |  |  |  |  |
| Cuthbert |  |  |  |  |  |

Owner

N
W — E
S

2  3  4
———————
1    5

| House No | Cat | Owner |
|---|---|---|
|  |  |  |
|  |  |  |
|  |  |  |
|  |  |  |
|  |  |  |

# Poetry Place

The two men and three women who reside in the five houses seen on the map below don't live up to the name of their street, since none has a last name that rhymes with that of his or her first name. Can you discover not only their full names, but also where they all live?

**1** Penny lives further north than the person named Pugh, who lives further west than Ray.

**2** The woman named Tate lives directly opposite Terry; and they both live further north than Sue.

**3** The person named Day lives in a house with a number one higher than that of Terry's house.

| | First name | | | | | Last name | | | | |
|---|---|---|---|---|---|---|---|---|---|---|
| | Kate | Penny | Ray | Sue | Terry | Day | Perry | Pugh | Renny | Tate |
| No 1 | | | | | | | | | | |
| No 2 | | | | | | | | | | |
| No 3 | | | | | | | | | | |
| No 4 | | | | | | | | | | |
| No 5 | | | | | | | | | | |
| Day | | | | | | | | | | |
| Perry | | | | | | | | | | |
| Pugh | | | | | | | | | | |
| Renny | | | | | | | | | | |
| Tate | | | | | | | | | | |

| House No | First name | Last name |
|---|---|---|
| | | |
| | | |
| | | |
| | | |
| | | |

# The Patchwork Quilt

Mrs White is in the process of making a four-shade patchwork quilt. Each piece is either a square, or an upper or lower triangle, and so far she has stitched together twelve such pieces, each in one of the four shades. How is the quilt made up?

1  No piece is stitched along an entire edge to another piece of the same shade, although two or more pieces may touch at the very corners: so, for example, piece H may be of the same shade as piece I, but neither is of the same shade as piece C.

2  Piece B is of a different shade to piece H.

3  Piece C is orange.

4  Piece D is yellow.

5  Piece F is red.

6  Piece G is of a different shade to piece L.

| | Square | | | | Triangle (upper) | | | | Triangle (lower) | | | |
|---|---|---|---|---|---|---|---|---|---|---|---|---|
| | A | B | C | D | E | G | I | K | F | H | J | L |
| Green | | | | | | | | | | | | |
| Orange | | | | | | | | | | | | |
| Red | | | | | | | | | | | | |
| Yellow | | | | | | | | | | | | |
| Lower F | | | | | | | | | | | | |
| Lower H | | | | | | | | | | | | |
| Lower J | | | | | | | | | | | | |
| Lower L | | | | | | | | | | | | |
| Upper E | | | | | | | | | | | | |
| Upper G | | | | | | | | | | | | |
| Upper I | | | | | | | | | | | | |
| Upper K | | | | | | | | | | | | |

| Shade | Square | Triangle (upper) | Triangle (lower) |
|---|---|---|---|
| | | | |
| | | | |
| | | | |
| | | | |

# A Bunch of Dates

Four friends were all born on different dates in
different months and years. How old is each, and on
which date does he celebrate his birthday?

1 The 20-year-old's birthday occurs two months later in the year
than that of the person whose birthday falls later in its month
than Donny's birthday.

2 Donny is two years older than the friend whose birthday is the
month before Dougal's.

3 Dougal isn't the person whose birthday is on 13 September.

4 Darren's birthday occurs earlier in the year than that of the
person born on the 9th, but later in the year than that of the
22-year-old.

|  | Age | | | | Date | | | | Month | | | |
|---|---|---|---|---|---|---|---|---|---|---|---|---|
|  | 19 | 20 | 21 | 22 | 9th | 11th | 13th | 15th | June | July | August | September |
| Darren |  |  |  |  |  |  |  |  |  |  |  |  |
| Dean |  |  |  |  |  |  |  |  |  |  |  |  |
| Donny |  |  |  |  |  |  |  |  |  |  |  |  |
| Dougal |  |  |  |  |  |  |  |  |  |  |  |  |
| June |  |  |  |  |  |  |  |  |  |  |  |  |
| July |  |  |  |  |  |  |  |  |  |  |  |  |
| August |  |  |  |  |  |  |  |  |  |  |  |  |
| September |  |  |  |  |  |  |  |  |  |  |  |  |
| 9th |  |  |  |  |  |  |  |  |  |  |  |  |
| 11th |  |  |  |  |  |  |  |  |  |  |  |  |
| 13th |  |  |  |  |  |  |  |  |  |  |  |  |
| 15th |  |  |  |  |  |  |  |  |  |  |  |  |

| Friend | Age | Date | Month |
|---|---|---|---|
|  |  |  |  |
|  |  |  |  |
|  |  |  |  |
|  |  |  |  |

# Potted Plants

Every day last week when she was at work, Fleur shopped at lunchtime, visiting the florists, at which she purchased a pot of bulbs. The pots are arranged on her windowsill, as you can see in the diagram below. What type of plant is growing in each, and on which day was it bought?

1 The lilies are growing in a pot next to that bought on Monday.

2 Tuesday's purchase is next to and right of the pot containing snowdrops.

3 The crocuses are sprouting in the pot which is next to and right of (and is of a different size to) the pot purchased on Wednesday.

4 Thursday's purchase (not of the hyacinths) was not of the pot which is furthest left.

5 The hyacinths are growing in the pot which is next to and right of (and is of a different size to) the pot bought on Friday.

|  | Crocuses | Hyacinths | Lilies | Snowdrops | Tulips | Monday | Tuesday | Wednesday | Thursday | Friday |
|---|---|---|---|---|---|---|---|---|---|---|
| Pot A |  |  |  |  |  |  |  |  |  |  |
| Pot B |  |  |  |  |  |  |  |  |  |  |
| Pot C |  |  |  |  |  |  |  |  |  |  |
| Pot D |  |  |  |  |  |  |  |  |  |  |
| Pot E |  |  |  |  |  |  |  |  |  |  |
| Monday |  |  |  |  |  |
| Tuesday |  |  |  |  |  |
| Wednesday |  |  |  |  |  |
| Thursday |  |  |  |  |  |
| Friday |  |  |  |  |  |

LEFT ⇐    RIGHT ⇒

A  B  C  D  E

| Pot | Plant | Bought |
|---|---|---|
|  |  |  |
|  |  |  |
|  |  |  |
|  |  |  |
|  |  |  |

**98**

# Kids and Puppies

The five children in this puzzle are the proud owners of puppies. Can you match every child to the name of his or her dog, as well as correctly work out the age of each child?

1 Quentin is two years older than Spot's owner, but younger than Wendy.

2 Benji's owner is one year older than Rebecca, but younger than Bob's owner.

3 Stephen is older than Towser's owner but younger than Rebecca.

|  | Puppy | | | | | Age | | | | |
|---|---|---|---|---|---|---|---|---|---|---|
|  | Benji | Bob | Rolf | Spot | Towser | 7 | 8 | 9 | 10 | 11 |
| Quentin |  |  |  |  |  |  |  |  |  |  |
| Rebecca |  |  |  |  |  |  |  |  |  |  |
| Stephen |  |  |  |  |  |  |  |  |  |  |
| Tim |  |  |  |  |  |  |  |  |  |  |
| Wendy |  |  |  |  |  |  |  |  |  |  |
| 7 years old |  |  |  |  |  |
| 8 years old |  |  |  |  |  |
| 9 years old |  |  |  |  |  |
| 10 years old |  |  |  |  |  |
| 11 years old |  |  |  |  |  |

| Child | Puppy | Age |
|---|---|---|
|  |  |  |
|  |  |  |
|  |  |  |
|  |  |  |
|  |  |  |

# The Boat Race

The four leading yachts in the Longriver Boat Race are approaching the finish. Can you match the yachts (as seen in the diagram below) to their names, as well as determine the shade of each boat's hull, and the year in which it was built?

1  The *Andromeda* is further ahead in the race than the *Saucy Sue* which, in turn, is further ahead in the race than the boat built two years earlier than the *Andromeda*.

2  The vessel with the blue hull was built either three years earlier or three years later than the *Fandango*.

3  The *Jamboree* has a white hull, and is further ahead in the race than the yacht built two years later than the one with the green hull.

|  | Name | | | | Hull | | | | Year | | | |
|---|---|---|---|---|---|---|---|---|---|---|---|---|
|  | Andromeda | Fandango | Jamboree | Saucy Sue | Blue | Green | Red | White | 1998 | 2000 | 2002 | 2005 |
| Yacht A | | | | | | | | | | | | |
| Yacht B | | | | | | | | | | | | |
| Yacht C | | | | | | | | | | | | |
| Yacht D | | | | | | | | | | | | |
| 1998 | | | | | | | | | | | | |
| 2000 | | | | | | | | | | | | |
| 2002 | | | | | | | | | | | | |
| 2005 | | | | | | | | | | | | |
| Blue | | | | | | | | | | | | |
| Green | | | | | | | | | | | | |
| Red | | | | | | | | | | | | |
| White | | | | | | | | | | | | |

Direction of travel

A    B    C    D

| Yacht | Name | Hull | Year |
|---|---|---|---|
| | | | |
| | | | |
| | | | |
| | | | |

# Saving Up

Four couples who were married in different months last year are saving up their money, and doing part-time evening work to supplement their incomes, since each couple is planning to buy something substantial. Who are the husband and wife in each couple, when did they marry, and what are they saving for?

1 Neville and his wife were married two months before the couple who plan to take an extended vacation in Australia next year.

2 Dawn's husband's name begins with the same letter of the alphabet as that of the man who married the month before Dawn and her husband.

3 The couple who married in September are saving hard in order to buy their own house.

4 Kathy and her husband are keen sailors, and plan to buy their own boat. Kathy was married earlier in the year than Debbie, but later in the year than Terence.

5 Tommy and his wife aren't saving for a car.

|  | Wife | | | | Married | | | | Saving for | | | |
|---|---|---|---|---|---|---|---|---|---|---|---|---|
|  | Dawn | Debbie | Karen | Kathy | August | September | October | December | Boat | Car | House | Vacation |
| Neil |  |  |  |  |  |  |  |  |  |  |  |  |
| Neville |  |  |  |  |  |  |  |  |  |  |  |  |
| Terence |  |  |  |  |  |  |  |  |  |  |  |  |
| Tommy |  |  |  |  |  |  |  |  |  |  |  |  |
| Boat |  |  |  |  |  |  |  |  | | | | |
| Car |  |  |  |  |  |  |  |  | | | | |
| House |  |  |  |  |  |  |  |  | | | | |
| Vacation |  |  |  |  |  |  |  |  | | | | |
| August |  |  |  |  | | | | | | | | |
| September |  |  |  |  | | | | | | | | |
| October |  |  |  |  | | | | | | | | |
| December |  |  |  |  | | | | | | | | |

| Husband | Wife | Married | Saving for |
|---|---|---|---|
|  |  |  |  |
|  |  |  |  |
|  |  |  |  |
|  |  |  |  |

# Acting the Part

Five actresses attended an audition for a minor part in a musical, and each was asked to sing and dance before a small panel which consisted of the management team and a few entertainment critics. After all five women had performed, they were rated on their abilities in the order first to fifth. Can you discover how each woman was placed in both singing and dancing?

1. Jenny achieved a position two higher than Davina's in singing. Jenny's position in dancing was two lower than Tina's.

2. Tina's singing position was three places lower than her dancing position.

3. The woman rated in second position in singing was placed fifth in dancing.

4. Clarissa's dancing position was higher than Wyn's singing position.

| Actress | Singing | Dancing |
|---|---|---|
|  |  |  |
|  |  |  |
|  |  |  |
|  |  |  |
|  |  |  |

# Snacking at Work

Five men who share an office have made a decision to cut down on the number of candies and cookies each eats at work during the week. Can you discover how many candies and cookies each got through last week?

1 Jack ate exactly the same number of cookies as the number of candies eaten by Lee.

2 The man who ate four more cookies than Keith consumed the highest number of candies.

3 Lee ate fewer cookies than Martin, but more than Noel.

4 Keith ate fewer candies than Martin, but more than Noel.

| | Candies | | | | | Cookies | | | | |
|---|---|---|---|---|---|---|---|---|---|---|
| | 19 | 20 | 23 | 24 | 25 | 20 | 24 | 26 | 30 | 32 |
| Jack | | | | | | | | | | |
| Keith | | | | | | | | | | |
| Lee | | | | | | | | | | |
| Martin | | | | | | | | | | |
| Noel | | | | | | | | | | |
| 20 cookies | | | | | | | | | | |
| 24 cookies | | | | | | | | | | |
| 26 cookies | | | | | | | | | | |
| 30 cookies | | | | | | | | | | |
| 32 cookies | | | | | | | | | | |

| Name | Candies | Cookies |
|---|---|---|
| | | |
| | | |
| | | |
| | | |
| | | |

# Visitors

The four people in this puzzle recently spent varying amounts of time with friends and relations. Who did each visit, on what day last month did the visit start, and for how long did he or she stay?

**1** Charlotte returned home on the 25th, but not after visiting her aunt.

**2** Whoever stayed with an aunt was away for two fewer days than the person whose visit to a friend started on the 11th of last month.

**3** Jessica's visit was shorter (and took place later in the month) than Victor's visit. Jessica didn't visit her grandfather.

|  | Visited | | | | Date | | | | Stayed for | | | |
|---|---|---|---|---|---|---|---|---|---|---|---|---|
|  | Aunt | Cousin | Friend | Grandfather | 2nd | 6th | 11th | 18th | 5 days | 7 days | 9 days | 11 days |
| Charlotte |  |  |  |  |  |  |  |  |  |  |  |  |
| Jessica |  |  |  |  |  |  |  |  |  |  |  |  |
| Norman |  |  |  |  |  |  |  |  |  |  |  |  |
| Victor |  |  |  |  |  |  |  |  |  |  |  |  |
| 5 days |  |  |  |  |  |  |  |  |
| 7 days |  |  |  |  |  |  |  |  |
| 9 days |  |  |  |  |  |  |  |  |
| 11 days |  |  |  |  |  |  |  |  |
| 2nd |  |  |  |  |
| 6th |  |  |  |  |
| 11th |  |  |  |  |
| 18th |  |  |  |  |

| Visitor | Visited | Date | Stayed |
|---|---|---|---|
|  |  |  |  |
|  |  |  |  |
|  |  |  |  |
|  |  |  |  |

# Labrador Dog Show

There were four finalists in this year's Little Lake Labrador Show. Can you match each dog to its owner, age, and finishing position at the end of the final round?

1 The youngest dog finished in a lower position than a dog with the same number of letters in its name as that of the dog which belongs to Mr Gray.

2 Max belongs to Mr Cheeseman and is seven months older than the dog that finished in second place.

3 Cleo finished in a higher position (and is younger) than Mrs Lester's dog.

4 Mr Gray's dog is older than the dog that finished in first place.

5 Glen finished in a higher position than at least one other dog.

|  | Owner | | | | Age | | | | Position | | | |
|---|---|---|---|---|---|---|---|---|---|---|---|---|
|  | Mr Cheeseman | Mr Gray | Mrs Lester | Mrs Turton | 15 months | 18 months | 22 months | 25 months | First | Second | Third | Fourth |
| Cleo | | | | | | | | | | | | |
| Glen | | | | | | | | | | | | |
| Max | | | | | | | | | | | | |
| Tim | | | | | | | | | | | | |
| First | | | | | | | | | |
| Second | | | | | | | | | |
| Third | | | | | | | | | |
| Fourth | | | | | | | | | |
| 15 months | | | | | |
| 18 months | | | | | |
| 22 months | | | | | |
| 25 months | | | | | |

| Dog | Owner | Age | Position |
|---|---|---|---|
| | | | |
| | | | |
| | | | |
| | | | |

# The Vegetable Garden

**105**

Arnie has a large vegetable garden, in which he is growing five different types of vegetables this year. The garden is divided into ten sections (see plan below), and he intends to use two sections for each type of vegetable. Which two sections will be used for each, given that no two sections containing the same vegetable will be on the same side of the path as each other?

1  The section of beans to the west of the path has a higher number than the section of beans to the east of the path.

2  Both the section of carrots and the section of potatoes to the west of the path have a higher number than the section of onions to the east of the path.

3  The section of lettuce to the east of the path has a lower number than the section of potatoes to the west of the path (which aren't to be grown in sections 5 or 9).

4  The section of carrots to the east of the path has a lower number than the section of onions to the west of the path, which won't be sown in an adjacent section to that of the potatoes.

|          | West side |   |   |   |   | East side |   |   |   |    |
|----------|---|---|---|---|---|---|---|---|---|----|
|          | 1 | 3 | 5 | 7 | 9 | 2 | 4 | 6 | 8 | 10 |
| Beans    |   |   |   |   |   |   |   |   |   |    |
| Carrots  |   |   |   |   |   |   |   |   |   |    |
| Lettuce  |   |   |   |   |   |   |   |   |   |    |
| Onions   |   |   |   |   |   |   |   |   |   |    |
| Potatoes |   |   |   |   |   |   |   |   |   |    |
| 2        |   |   |   |   |   |   |   |   |   |    |
| 4        |   |   |   |   |   |   |   |   |   |    |
| 6        |   |   |   |   |   |   |   |   |   |    |
| 8        |   |   |   |   |   |   |   |   |   |    |
| 10       |   |   |   |   |   |   |   |   |   |    |

East side (vertical label on left of lower grid)

| 1 | SHED | 2  |
|---|------|----|
| 3 | P    | 4  |
| 5 | A    | 6  |
| 7 | T    | 8  |
| 9 | H    | 10 |

| Vegetable | West side | East side |
|-----------|-----------|-----------|
|           |           |           |
|           |           |           |
|           |           |           |
|           |           |           |
|           |           |           |

# Amateur Golfers

The five men who appear in this puzzle are all representing different provinces at the next Canadian Amateur Golfing Championships (other golfers are taking part, of course, but this puzzle doesn't feature them!). Can you work out which province each will represent, and his personal best drive to date?

1 The personal best drive of the man from Manitoba is twenty yards further than that of the man from Nova Scotia.

2 Frank's best drive to date is thirty yards further than that of the golfer representing Quebec.

3 Albert (who represents Ontario) has a personal best drive which is ten yards further than that of the man representing Alberta.

4 Larry's personal best drive is either twenty or thirty yards further than Neil's personal best drive.

| | Province | | | | | Best drive | | | | |
|---|---|---|---|---|---|---|---|---|---|---|
| | Alberta | Manitoba | Nova Scotia | Ontario | Quebec | 280 yards | 290 yards | 300 yards | 320 yards | 330 yards |
| Albert | | | | | | | | | | |
| Frank | | | | | | | | | | |
| James | | | | | | | | | | |
| Larry | | | | | | | | | | |
| Neil | | | | | | | | | | |
| 280 yards | | | | | | | | | | |
| 290 yards | | | | | | | | | | |
| 300 yards | | | | | | | | | | |
| 320 yards | | | | | | | | | | |
| 330 yards | | | | | | | | | | |

| Golfer | Province | Best drive |
|---|---|---|
| | | |
| | | |
| | | |
| | | |
| | | |

# Suns, Moons, and Stars

Four children painted pictures of outer space (as they see it!), and have arranged them as you see in the diagram below. Can you decide how many suns, moons, and stars feature in each picture, given that there are three different quantities of each in every painting?

1 The picture with four suns has as many stars as the number of moons which feature in the picture with six stars.

2 The picture with five suns is further left than the one with seven stars, but further right than the one with four moons.

3 The picture with five stars has three more moons than picture C.

|  | Suns | | | | Moons | | | | Stars | | | |
|---|---|---|---|---|---|---|---|---|---|---|---|---|
|  | 3 | 4 | 5 | 7 | 3 | 4 | 6 | 7 | 3 | 5 | 6 | 7 |
| Picture A |  |  |  |  |  |  |  |  |  |  |  |  |
| Picture B |  |  |  |  |  |  |  |  |  |  |  |  |
| Picture C |  |  |  |  |  |  |  |  |  |  |  |  |
| Picture D |  |  |  |  |  |  |  |  |  |  |  |  |
| 3 stars |  |  |  |  |  |  |  |  | | | | |
| 5 stars |  |  |  |  |  |  |  |  | | | | |
| 6 stars |  |  |  |  |  |  |  |  | | | | |
| 7 stars |  |  |  |  |  |  |  |  | | | | |
| 3 moons |  |  |  |  | | | | | | | | |
| 4 moons |  |  |  |  | | | | | | | | |
| 6 moons |  |  |  |  | | | | | | | | |
| 7 moons |  |  |  |  | | | | | | | | |

LEFT ⇦          RIGHT ⇨

| A | B | C | D |

| Picture | Suns | Moons | Stars |
|---|---|---|---|
|  |  |  |  |
|  |  |  |  |
|  |  |  |  |
|  |  |  |  |

# Shopping Spree

Phil and Phoebe are getting married soon, and went shopping yesterday to buy things for their new home. Discover the order in which they went into each store, together with the name of the assistant who served them, and the item they bought there.

1  The bed was bought earlier than the item sold to Phil and Phoebe at Shop Rite, but later than the item sold to them by Peter.

2  Phil and Phoebe visited Downton's directly after buying a pair of drapes.

3  Stan served Phil and Phoebe in the store visited directly before the one where Geraldine works. Stan doesn't work at Lo Cost.

4  The freezer was sold to Phil and Phoebe by Angela, but not at the store visited last.

5  Wize Buys wasn't the store visited third. Angela doesn't work at Wize Buys.

|  | Order | | | | Assistant | | | | Bought | | | |
|---|---|---|---|---|---|---|---|---|---|---|---|---|
|  | First | Second | Third | Fourth | Angela | Geraldine | Peter | Stan | Bed | Drapes | Freezer | Table |
| Downton's | | | | | | | | | | | | |
| Lo Cost | | | | | | | | | | | | |
| Shop Rite | | | | | | | | | | | | |
| Wize Buys | | | | | | | | | | | | |
| Bed | | | | | | | | | | | | |
| Drapes | | | | | | | | | | | | |
| Freezer | | | | | | | | | | | | |
| Table | | | | | | | | | | | | |
| Angela | | | | | | | | | | | | |
| Geraldine | | | | | | | | | | | | |
| Peter | | | | | | | | | | | | |
| Stan | | | | | | | | | | | | |

| Shop | Order | Assistant | Bought |
|---|---|---|---|
| | | | |
| | | | |
| | | | |
| | | | |

# On Vacation

Each of the five people in this puzzle is lucky enough to be able to afford two vacations every year. They've already had one, skiing in January – and now they're all enjoying another. Can you discover the country in which each skied, as well as that in which they are now on vacation?

1  No person is currently in a country in which he or she skied in January.

2  Kevin is currently in France and the person who skied in France is currently in Spain.

3  No-one has visited both Canada and Scotland this year.

4  Jodi skied in Italy in January, but isn't the person now on vacation in Canada. Toby didn't ski in the country in which Jodi is now enjoying herself.

5  Toby and William both skied in countries which have names that begin with the same letter of the alphabet.

|  | Skied in | | | | | Now in | | | | |
|---|---|---|---|---|---|---|---|---|---|---|
|  | Canada | France | Italy | Scotland | Switzerland | Canada | France | Norway | Scotland | Spain |
| Jodi |  |  |  |  |  |  |  |  |  |  |
| Kevin |  |  |  |  |  |  |  |  |  |  |
| Marcia |  |  |  |  |  |  |  |  |  |  |
| Toby |  |  |  |  |  |  |  |  |  |  |
| William |  |  |  |  |  |  |  |  |  |  |
| Canada |  |  |  |  |  |
| France |  |  |  |  |  |
| Norway |  |  |  |  |  |
| Scotland |  |  |  |  |  |
| Spain |  |  |  |  |  |

(Now in)

| Name | Skied in | Now in |
|---|---|---|
|  |  |  |
|  |  |  |
|  |  |  |
|  |  |  |
|  |  |  |

# Hide and Seek

Six children played a game of hide and seek. Leanne was chosen as the first seeker, so closed her eyes and counted to 100 before trying to find the others. Where had they all hidden, and how long was it before Leanne found each child?

**1** Fiona took longer to find than the child (not Sally) who hid behind a rock.

**2** The child who hid in a shed took two fewer minutes to find than the one who decided to hide in the branches of an apple tree.

**3** Gayle squeezed under an old bush and was found in less time than it took to locate the child who hid behind a tree. Robert didn't hide behind anything.

**4** It took Leanne three minutes longer to find Benjamin than it took her to find Sally.

|  | Behind a rock | Behind a tree | In a shed | Under a bush | Up a tree | 2 | 3 | 4 | 5 | 6 |
|---|---|---|---|---|---|---|---|---|---|---|
| **Place** | | | | | | **Time (mins)** | | | | |
| Benjamin | | | | | | | | | | |
| Fiona | | | | | | | | | | |
| Gayle | | | | | | | | | | |
| Robert | | | | | | | | | | |
| Sally | | | | | | | | | | |
| 2 minutes | | | | | | | | | | |
| 3 minutes | | | | | | | | | | |
| 4 minutes | | | | | | | | | | |
| 5 minutes | | | | | | | | | | |
| 6 minutes | | | | | | | | | | |

| Hider | Place | Time |
|---|---|---|
| | | |
| | | |
| | | |
| | | |
| | | |

# Playing Pete

Private investigator Pete Prior is a popular fictional detective, and four movies of his exploits have exceeded box office expectations in recent years. What is the first name and last name of the man who played the part of Pete Prior in each movie, and in which year was the movie released?

1 Alan Bourne once played the part of Pete Prior, but not in *Dead Ringer*, which was released two years before *Forget Her*.

2 Mr Montgomery played the rôle of Pete Prior two years before Neil did so.

3 Frank didn't feature in the 2003 film. However, he played the part of Pete Prior in an earlier year than Graham, whose last name isn't Fontaine.

4 The actor named Steele didn't play the lead rôle in *His Final Word*.

|  | Actor | | | | Last name | | | | Year | | | |
|---|---|---|---|---|---|---|---|---|---|---|---|---|
|  | Alan | Frank | Graham | Neil | Bourne | Fontaine | Montgomery | Steele | 2003 | 2005 | 2006 | 2007 |
| Cold Case | | | | | | | | | | | | |
| Dead Ringer | | | | | | | | | | | | |
| Forget Her | | | | | | | | | | | | |
| His Final Word | | | | | | | | | | | | |
| 2003 | | | | | | | | | | | | |
| 2005 | | | | | | | | | | | | |
| 2006 | | | | | | | | | | | | |
| 2007 | | | | | | | | | | | | |
| Bourne | | | | | | | | | | | | |
| Fontaine | | | | | | | | | | | | |
| Montgomery | | | | | | | | | | | | |
| Steele | | | | | | | | | | | | |

| Movie | Actor | Last name | Year |
|---|---|---|---|
|  |  |  |  |
|  |  |  |  |
|  |  |  |  |
|  |  |  |  |

# A Drink Problem

Last weekend, the four people in this puzzle decided to restock their cellars with beer and wine. Everyone spent different amounts on these two drinks, buying different quantities. Your task is to determine each shopper's name, and the amount of money he or she spent on beer and wine.

1 The person named Samson spent five dollars more than Lisa on beer.

2 Lisa spent more on wine than the person named Harper, who spent less on beer than Tony.

3 Tony spent more on wine than the person named Taylor.

4 Whoever spent $35 on beer spent less on wine than Annabel.

5 Scott spent either eight or ten dollars less on wine than the person named Barber.

6 The person named Barber didn't spend five dollars more than Scott on beer.

| | Last name | | | | Beer | | | | Wine | | | |
|---|---|---|---|---|---|---|---|---|---|---|---|---|
| | Barber | Harper | Samson | Taylor | $25 | $30 | $35 | $40 | $30 | $38 | $42 | $48 |
| Annabel | | | | | | | | | | | | |
| Lisa | | | | | | | | | | | | |
| Scott | | | | | | | | | | | | |
| Tony | | | | | | | | | | | | |
| Wine $30 | | | | | | | | | | | | |
| Wine $38 | | | | | | | | | | | | |
| Wine $42 | | | | | | | | | | | | |
| Wine $48 | | | | | | | | | | | | |
| Beer $25 | | | | | | | | | | | | |
| Beer $30 | | | | | | | | | | | | |
| Beer $35 | | | | | | | | | | | | |
| Beer $40 | | | | | | | | | | | | |

| Shopper | Last name | Beer | Wine |
|---|---|---|---|
| | | | |
| | | | |
| | | | |
| | | | |

# Piggy Banks

The five children in this puzzle all have two piggy banks:
a day-to-day piggy bank and one where they save money to
spend on an annual family vacation. Can you discover how
much (to the nearest dollar) each has in his or her two boxes?

1  The child with $13 in his or her day-to-day piggy bank has saved
   more towards the vacation than Kenny, but less towards the
   vacation than Victoria.

2  Comparing their vacation piggy banks, Stephen has one dollar
   more than Patricia. However, in their day-to day piggy banks,
   Stephen has one fewer dollar than Patricia.

3  In both of her piggy banks, Victoria has less money than Bruce.

4  The combined total of the amounts in Kenny's two boxes is one
   dollar more than the combined total of the amounts in Victoria's
   two boxes.

|  | Day-to-day | | | | | Vacation | | | | |
|---|---|---|---|---|---|---|---|---|---|---|
|  | $10 | $12 | $13 | $15 | $16 | $22 | $23 | $24 | $26 | $27 |
| Bruce |  |  |  |  |  |  |  |  |  |  |
| Kenny |  |  |  |  |  |  |  |  |  |  |
| Patricia |  |  |  |  |  |  |  |  |  |  |
| Stephen |  |  |  |  |  |  |  |  |  |  |
| Victoria |  |  |  |  |  |  |  |  |  |  |
| Holiday $22 |  |  |  |  |  |
| Holiday $23 |  |  |  |  |  |
| Holiday $24 |  |  |  |  |  |
| Holiday $26 |  |  |  |  |  |
| Holiday $27 |  |  |  |  |  |

| Child | Day-to-day | Vacation |
|---|---|---|
|  |  |  |
|  |  |  |
|  |  |  |
|  |  |  |
|  |  |  |

# Decorating Session

John has decided that the inside of his apartment needs freshening up a little, so he went out this morning to buy cans of paint, in order that he can redecorate five rooms over the course of the next few weeks. Every week he intends to paint a different room, but can you discover when, and with which paint?

1   John will be repainting his bedroom earlier than his lounge.

2   The lemon paint will be used the week before the bathroom is freshened up, but the week after the lime green paint.

3   The kitchen is to be painted cream and John will undertake this work earlier than the repainting of the hallway, a job he doesn't intend to do in week 4. The lime green paint isn't for the hallway.

4   The white paint will be used earlier than the paint John has chosen for his bathroom.

|  | Bathroom | Bedroom | Hallway | Kitchen | Lounge | Cream | Lemon | Lime | Pale blue | White |
|---|---|---|---|---|---|---|---|---|---|---|
| **Room** | | | | | | **Paint** | | | | |
| Week 1 | | | | | | | | | | |
| Week 2 | | | | | | | | | | |
| Week 3 | | | | | | | | | | |
| Week 4 | | | | | | | | | | |
| Week 5 | | | | | | | | | | |
| Cream | | | | | | | | | | |
| Lemon | | | | | | | | | | |
| Lime | | | | | | | | | | |
| Pale blue | | | | | | | | | | |
| White | | | | | | | | | | |

| Week | Room | Paint |
|---|---|---|
| | | |
| | | |
| | | |
| | | |
| | | |

# Artists in the Making

Four would-be artists sat at easels numbered 1-4 in a local art class. Each used a different medium and chose a different subject. Discover the facts by studying the clues below.

1 The horse was the subject of the artist who sat at an easel with a number one higher than that used by Ronald, but one lower than that of the person (not Thelma) who chose water-based paint for his or her picture.

2 The artist who used pencils (whose chosen subject wasn't the dog) sat at an easel with a number one lower than that of the person whose subject was the forest.

3 Oil paints were chosen for the mountain scene painted by the artist who sat at an easel with a number two higher than that at which Harriet sat.

|  | Easel No | | | | Medium | | | | Subject | | | |
|---|---|---|---|---|---|---|---|---|---|---|---|---|
|  | 1 | 2 | 3 | 4 | Oils | Pastels | Pencils | Water-based | Dog | Forest | Horse | Mountain |
| Charles |  |  |  |  |  |  |  |  |  |  |  |  |
| Harriet |  |  |  |  |  |  |  |  |  |  |  |  |
| Ronald |  |  |  |  |  |  |  |  |  |  |  |  |
| Thelma |  |  |  |  |  |  |  |  |  |  |  |  |
| Dog |  |  |  |  |  |  |  |  |  |  |  |  |
| Forest |  |  |  |  |  |  |  |  |  |  |  |  |
| Horse |  |  |  |  |  |  |  |  |  |  |  |  |
| Mountain |  |  |  |  |  |  |  |  |  |  |  |  |
| Oils |  |  |  |  |  |  |  |  |  |  |  |  |
| Pastels |  |  |  |  |  |  |  |  |  |  |  |  |
| Pencils |  |  |  |  |  |  |  |  |  |  |  |  |
| Water-based |  |  |  |  |  |  |  |  |  |  |  |  |

| Artist | Easel No |
|---|---|
|  |  |
|  |  |
|  |  |
|  |  |

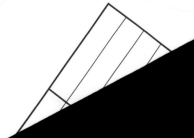

120

# Collectors' Fairs

Since as far back as she can recall, Louise has had an interest in collecting old things, and regularly visits Collectors' Fairs in the hope of obtaining an item or two. Last year she attended four, each in a different season. Can you discover the location of every fair, the subject of each, and the amount Louise spent there?

1 Louise spent $100 more on kitchenware than she spent at the Spring Fair.

2 It wasn't at the Summer Fair that Louise indulged her passion for collecting old clothes. The Winter Fair wasn't held in Regina.

3 Two handmade maps caught Louise's eye in Winnipeg, and she spent $200 less on these items than she spent the previous season at the Fair held in Saskatoon.

4 The Fair in Edmonton was held earlier in the year than the Fair (not in Winnipeg) where Louise spent a total of $100.

|  | Location | | | | Subject | | | | Spent | | | |
|---|---|---|---|---|---|---|---|---|---|---|---|---|
|  | Edmonton | Regina | Saskatoon | Winnipeg | Clothing | Kitchenware | Maps | Paintings | $100 | $200 | $300 | $400 |
| Spring |  |  |  |  |  |  |  |  |  |  |  |  |
| Summer |  |  |  |  |  |  |  |  |  |  |  |  |
| Autumn |  |  |  |  |  |  |  |  |  |  |  |  |
| Winter |  |  |  |  |  |  |  |  |  |  |  |  |
| $100 |  |  |  |  |  |  |  |  | | | | |
| $200 |  |  |  |  |  |  |  |  | | | | |
| $300 |  |  |  |  |  |  |  |  | | | | |
| $400 |  |  |  |  |  |  |  |  | | | | |
| Clothing |  |  |  |  | | | | | | | | |
| Kitchenware |  |  |  |  | | | | | | | | |
| Maps |  |  |  |  | | | | | | | | |
| Paintings |  |  |  |  | | | | | | | | |

| Season | Location | Subject | Spent |
|---|---|---|---|
|  |  |  |  |
|  |  |  |  |
|  |  |  |  |
|  |  |  |  |

# Alien Races

In a distant solar system, eight planets orbit a sun very much like our own. However, five of these planets are inhabited by creatures like none to be found on Earth. Can you discover the name of each planet as shown on the map below, and name the dominant race living on each?

1 The Croptils live on a planet further from the sun than Alpten which, in turn, is further from the sun than the planet the Ermings call home.

2 There are two planets between the orbits of Patnel and Naptle: that on which the Arinoms live, and Lanpet.

3 The Brovides live closer to the sun than the planet Entlap, but further from the sun than the Croptils' home planet.

4 The Brovides' home planet is not Naptle.

| | Name | | | | | Dominant Race | | | | |
|---|---|---|---|---|---|---|---|---|---|---|
| | Alpten | Entlap | Lanpet | Patnel | Naptle | Arinoms | Brovides | Croptils | Dembles | Ermings |
| Planet A | | | | | | | | | | |
| Planet B | | | | | | | | | | |
| Planet C | | | | | | | | | | |
| Planet D | | | | | | | | | | |
| Planet E | | | | | | | | | | |
| Arinoms | | | | | | | | | | |
| Brovides | | | | | | | | | | |
| Croptils | | | | | | | | | | |
| Dembles | | | | | | | | | | |
| Ermings | | | | | | | | | | |

| Planet | Name | Race |
|---|---|---|
| | | |
| | | |
| | | |
| | | |
| | | |

# Split Personalities

One rainy day, Rachel became bored, so took photographs of five members of her family, and cut each into three pieces (head, body and legs), and then reassembled them in such a way that each "new" picture contains pieces of three "old" ones. How have the pictures been reassembled?

1. Rachel's mother's head is now attached to her father's body, which isn't in the same picture as Rachel's brother's legs.

2. Rachel's brother's body is now attached to her sister's legs.

3. Rachel's brother's legs aren't in the same picture as their mother's body, and neither her mother's body nor her brother's legs are in the same picture as Rachel's sister's head.

4. Rachel's father's head is not now attached to her sister's body.

|  |  | Body | | | | | Legs | | | | |
|---|---|---|---|---|---|---|---|---|---|---|---|
|  |  | Aunt | Brother | Father | Mother | Sister | Aunt | Brother | Father | Mother | Sister |
| Head | Aunt |  |  |  |  |  |  |  |  |  |  |
|  | Brother |  |  |  |  |  |  |  |  |  |  |
|  | Father |  |  |  |  |  |  |  |  |  |  |
|  | Mother |  |  |  |  |  |  |  |  |  |  |
|  | Sister |  |  |  |  |  |  |  |  |  |  |
| Legs | Aunt |  |  |  |  |  |  |  |  |  |  |
|  | Brother |  |  |  |  |  |  |  |  |  |  |
|  | Father |  |  |  |  |  |  |  |  |  |  |
|  | Mother |  |  |  |  |  |  |  |  |  |  |
|  | Sister |  |  |  |  |  |  |  |  |  |  |

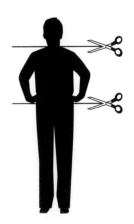

| Head | Body | Legs |
|---|---|---|
|  |  |  |
|  |  |  |
|  |  |  |
|  |  |  |
|  |  |  |

# Word Games

Four friends took the word NEWSPAPER, and challenged each other to find one four-letter word beginning with S, one four-letter word beginning with W, and any five-lettered word made from the letters in NEWSPAPER. They all managed to do this, and there were no duplications of any word. Can you discover the three words every person found?

1  Of three of the friends: one is the person who found both SWAP and WRAP; one is the person who found both WASP and SPREE; and one is Olivia.

2  Of three of the friends: one is the person who found both SEWN and PREEN; one is the person who found both WANE and SWEEP; and one is Neil.

3  Of three of the friends: one is Mary; one is Peter (who didn't find WANE); and one is the person who found WARN.

4  Of three of the friends: one is the person who found SNAP; one is Mary; and one is Peter.

|  | S word | | | | W word | | | | Five letters | | | |
|---|---|---|---|---|---|---|---|---|---|---|---|---|
|  | SEWN | SNAP | SPAN | SWAP | WANE | WARN | WASP | WRAP | NEWER | PREEN | SPREE | SWEEP |
| Mary |  |  |  |  |  |  |  |  |  |  |  |  |
| Neil |  |  |  |  |  |  |  |  |  |  |  |  |
| Olivia |  |  |  |  |  |  |  |  |  |  |  |  |
| Peter |  |  |  |  |  |  |  |  |  |  |  |  |
| NEWER |  |  |  |  |  |  |  |  |  |  |  |  |
| PREEN |  |  |  |  |  |  |  |  |  |  |  |  |
| SPREE |  |  |  |  |  |  |  |  |  |  |  |  |
| SWEEP |  |  |  |  |  |  |  |  |  |  |  |  |
| WANE |  |  |  |  |  |  |  |  |  |  |  |  |
| WARN |  |  |  |  |  |  |  |  |  |  |  |  |
| WASP |  |  |  |  |  |  |  |  |  |  |  |  |
| WRAP |  |  |  |  |  |  |  |  |  |  |  |  |

| Friend | S word | W word | Five letters |
|---|---|---|---|
|  |  |  |  |
|  |  |  |  |
|  |  |  |  |
|  |  |  |  |

# Keeping Appointments

While involved in activities they were enjoying, the four children who feature in this puzzle were interrupted by their mothers, who wanted to take them elsewhere. In what activity had each child been engrossed, what is the name of his or her mother, and who did they have an appointment to see?

1. The boy who was watching cartoons on television had an appointment with the optician, for an eye test.
2. Anna helped her daughter to tidy away the painting things before they left the house, promising her she could complete the painting later.
3. Corinne's child (not Mitch) was taken to see the hairdresser at the same time as Alison had a lesson with her piano tutor.
4. Naomi had been reading a book when she was called by her mother (not Mary), who took her to see the doctor.

|  | Modelmaking | Painting | Reading | Watching TV | Anna | Corinne | Leonie | Mary | Doctor | Hairdresser | Optician | Piano tutor |
|---|---|---|---|---|---|---|---|---|---|---|---|---|
| Alison | | | | | | | | | | | | |
| Barry | | | | | | | | | | | | |
| Mitch | | | | | | | | | | | | |
| Naomi | | | | | | | | | | | | |
| Doctor | | | | | | | | | | | | |
| Hairdresser | | | | | | | | | | | | |
| Optician | | | | | | | | | | | | |
| Piano tutor | | | | | | | | | | | | |
| Anna | | | | | | | | | | | | |
| Corinne | | | | | | | | | | | | |
| Leonie | | | | | | | | | | | | |
| Mary | | | | | | | | | | | | |

| Child | Activity | Mother | With |
|---|---|---|---|
| | | | |
| | | | |
| | | | |
| | | | |

# Gifts to Charity

**Gifts to Charity**

While in the shopping mall this morning, the five people in this puzzle each bought a sticker from a volunteer who was selling them in aid of charity. To which type of charity did each shopper make his or her donation, and who was the volunteer collector in each case?

1 Rodney (who didn't buy a sticker from either Honor or Verity) supported the charity in aid of sick animals.

2 Jimmy (who didn't donate to the charity protecting birds and their habitats) gave to a collector whose name begins with "H".

3 The sticker sold in aid of the blind wasn't given to Josephine.

4 Josephine didn't buy a sticker from Faith, who was collecting on behalf of war widows.

5 The sticker sold in aid of the blind was either bought from Verity or Charity (who received a donation from Brian).

| Shopper | Charity | Collector |
|---|---|---|
|  |  |  |
|  |  |  |
|  |  |  |
|  |  |  |
|  |  |  |

125

# A Busy Time

Donna has a hectic social calendar. Next week she will attend social functions on every weekday evening. Can you discover which evening, and at what time each event is scheduled to take place?

1 The trip to the movie is scheduled to start earlier in the evening than both the Thursday and Friday evening events.

2 The fashion show is taking place on Tuesday and starts at a later time than the dinner party (which isn't on Friday).

3 The bowling will be held two evenings earlier than the event that starts at half past six.

4 The bridge party starts three quarters of an hour later than Monday evening's event.

|  | Monday | Tuesday | Wednesday | Thursday | Friday | 6.30 pm | 6.45 pm | 7.00 pm | 7.15 pm | 7.30 pm |
|---|---|---|---|---|---|---|---|---|---|---|
| Bowling |  |  |  |  |  |  |  |  |  |  |
| Bridge party |  |  |  |  |  |  |  |  |  |  |
| Dinner party |  |  |  |  |  |  |  |  |  |  |
| Fashion show |  |  |  |  |  |  |  |  |  |  |
| Movie trip |  |  |  |  |  |  |  |  |  |  |
| 6.30 pm |  |  |  |  |  |
| 6.45 pm |  |  |  |  |  |
| 7.00 pm |  |  |  |  |  |
| 7.15 pm |  |  |  |  |  |
| 7.30 pm |  |  |  |  |  |

| Event | Evening | Time |
|---|---|---|
|  |  |  |
|  |  |  |
|  |  |  |
|  |  |  |
|  |  |  |

# Octogenarians

The four couples in this puzzle are all in their eighties. Can you discover who is married to whom, and their respective ages?

1 Arthur is of the same age as his wife.
2 Beth is older than her husband.
3 Richard is older than his wife.
4 Leonie is two years older than Mary.
5 Noelle is two years older than Vince.
6 Lenny is two years older than Richard.

| | Wife | | | | His age | | | | Her age | | | |
|---|---|---|---|---|---|---|---|---|---|---|---|---|
| | Beth | Leonie | Mary | Noelle | 83 | 84 | 85 | 87 | 81 | 83 | 85 | 86 |
| Arthur | | | | | | | | | | | | |
| Lenny | | | | | | | | | | | | |
| Richard | | | | | | | | | | | | |
| Vince | | | | | | | | | | | | |
| Her age 81 | | | | | | | | | | | | |
| Her age 83 | | | | | | | | | | | | |
| Her age 85 | | | | | | | | | | | | |
| Her age 86 | | | | | | | | | | | | |
| His age 83 | | | | | | | | | | | | |
| His age 84 | | | | | | | | | | | | |
| His age 85 | | | | | | | | | | | | |
| His age 87 | | | | | | | | | | | | |

| Husband | Wife | His age | Her age |
|---|---|---|---|
| | | | |
| | | | |
| | | | |
| | | | |

# Valentine Cards

The four sisters in this puzzle each received a Valentine card from a different admirer on February 14th last. The cards were lined up as you see them in the picture below. Can you work out to whom the cards were sent, as well as by whom, and also discover the age of each sister?

1. The youngest of the four sisters (whose card wasn't from Ralph) was sent the card that is next to and right of Myra's.

2. Roger sent a card to the girl who is one year older than the girl to whom Reuben's card was addressed.

3. The card sent by Rupert is next to and between the one sent to the 16-year-old and the one sent to Jill.

4. The recipient of card A is older than Clarissa, who is older than the sister who received the card directly next to and right of Clarissa's.

5. Penny's card is further left than at least one other.

|  | Sister | | | | Admirer | | | | Her age | | | |
|---|---|---|---|---|---|---|---|---|---|---|---|---|
|  | Clarissa | Jill | Myra | Penny | Ralph | Reuben | Roger | Rupert | 16 | 17 | 19 | 20 |
| Card A |  |  |  |  |  |  |  |  |  |  |  |  |
| Card B |  |  |  |  |  |  |  |  |  |  |  |  |
| Card C |  |  |  |  |  |  |  |  |  |  |  |  |
| Card D |  |  |  |  |  |  |  |  |  |  |  |  |
| 16 years old |  |  |  |  |  |  |  |  |  |  |  |  |
| 17 years old |  |  |  |  |  |  |  |  |  |  |  |  |
| 19 years old |  |  |  |  |  |  |  |  |  |  |  |  |
| 20 years old |  |  |  |  |  |  |  |  |  |  |  |  |
| Ralph |  |  |  |  |  |  |  |  |  |  |  |  |
| Reuben |  |  |  |  |  |  |  |  |  |  |  |  |
| Roger |  |  |  |  |  |  |  |  |  |  |  |  |
| Rupert |  |  |  |  |  |  |  |  |  |  |  |  |

**LEFT** ⇦        **RIGHT** ⇨

A  B  C  D

| Card | Sister | Admirer | Her age |
|---|---|---|---|
|  |  |  |  |
|  |  |  |  |
|  |  |  |  |
|  |  |  |  |

# Currency Exchange

Five British people have just collected their foreign currency
from the Bureau de Change in town. Each has dollars,
but all are going to different countries, so their dollars are
all different! Can you discover how much money each
has, and the country to which he or she is going?

**1** Hal (who isn't going to the United States of America) has twice
as much money as the person going to New Zealand.

**2** The person journeying to Australia has $800.

**3** The person going to Singapore has $200 more than Graham.

**4** Frances has twice as much money as Lydia, who is going to
Canada.

|  | $ 300 | $ 500 | $ 600 | $ 800 | $1,000 | Australia | Canada | New Zealand | Singapore | USA |
|---|---|---|---|---|---|---|---|---|---|---|
| Frances |  |  |  |  |  |  |  |  |  |  |
| Graham |  |  |  |  |  |  |  |  |  |  |
| Hal |  |  |  |  |  |  |  |  |  |  |
| Lydia |  |  |  |  |  |  |  |  |  |  |
| Nancy |  |  |  |  |  |  |  |  |  |  |
| Australia |  |  |  |  |  |
| Canada |  |  |  |  |  |
| New Zealand |  |  |  |  |  |
| Singapore |  |  |  |  |  |
| USA |  |  |  |  |  |

| Name | Dollars | Country |
|---|---|---|
|  |  |  |
|  |  |  |
|  |  |  |
|  |  |  |
|  |  |  |

# Easter Eggs

The five women in this puzzle all bought Easter eggs – for themselves! What shade was the box containing each woman's purchase, and how much did she spend?

1 Roberta's egg cost fifty cents less than the egg in the attractive yellow box, which wasn't purchased by Verna.

2 The egg in the gold box cost more than the one in the silver box (which wasn't bought by Verna or Juliet).

3 Nadine paid more for her egg than Juliet, but less than the price of the egg in the blue box.

4 Verna paid fifty cents less for her egg than the price of the egg in the green box (which wasn't bought by Alison).

|  | Blue | Gold | Green | Silver | Yellow | $3.50 | $4.00 | $4.50 | $5.00 | $5.50 |
|---|---|---|---|---|---|---|---|---|---|---|
| Alison |  |  |  |  |  |  |  |  |  |  |
| Juliet |  |  |  |  |  |  |  |  |  |  |
| Nadine |  |  |  |  |  |  |  |  |  |  |
| Roberta |  |  |  |  |  |  |  |  |  |  |
| Verna |  |  |  |  |  |  |  |  |  |  |
| $3.50 |  |  |  |  |  |
| $4.00 |  |  |  |  |  |
| $4.50 |  |  |  |  |  |
| $5.00 |  |  |  |  |  |
| $5.50 |  |  |  |  |  |

| Buyer | Box | Price |
|---|---|---|
|  |  |  |
|  |  |  |
|  |  |  |
|  |  |  |
|  |  |  |

# Christmas Trees

Four of the residents of Advent Avenue placed Christmas trees in their gardens last year, each decorated with different tinsel, and with a different ornament on the top. Can you discover the number of the house at which each person lives, together with details of his or her tree?

1  The tree decorated with silver tinsel was in a garden further east than the one with a star on the top, but further west than the one decorated with a miniature Santa Claus.

2  The tree with silver tinsel wasn't that with a snowflake on the top, which was in the garden of the house next to and west of Norman's house, which is next to and west of the one decorated with blue tinsel.

3  Catherine's house (not No 7) is further from Johnny's house than it is from the house owned by the person whose tree was swathed in gold tinsel.

4  The tree with an angel on the top was in the garden of a house that is closer to Lavinia's than to the one owned by the person whose tree was hung with purple tinsel.

|  | House No | | | | Tinsel | | | | Ornament | | | |
|---|---|---|---|---|---|---|---|---|---|---|---|---|
|  | 1 | 3 | 5 | 7 | Blue | Gold | Purple | Silver | Angel | Santa | Snowflake | Star |
| Catherine | | | | | | | | | | | | |
| Johnny | | | | | | | | | | | | |
| Lavinia | | | | | | | | | | | | |
| Norman | | | | | | | | | | | | |
| Angel | | | | | | | | | | | | |
| Santa | | | | | | | | | | | | |
| Snowflake | | | | | | | | | | | | |
| Star | | | | | | | | | | | | |
| Blue | | | | | | | | | | | | |
| Gold | | | | | | | | | | | | |
| Purple | | | | | | | | | | | | |
| Silver | | | | | | | | | | | | |

WEST ⇐    EAST ⇒

No 1    No 3    No 5    No 7

| Resident | House | Tinsel | Ornament |
|---|---|---|---|
|  |  |  |  |
|  |  |  |  |
|  |  |  |  |
|  |  |  |  |

# Premium Payments

Four people each paid their annual premiums for car insurance, house insurance and life insurance over the course of the final five months of last year. No-one paid more than one premium per month but, nonetheless, all felt the financial strain on their wallets! Can you discover in which month each person paid the premiums?

1  Gordon paid his car insurance the month after he paid his life insurance.

2  Henry paid his house insurance in the same month that Tim paid his life insurance and Leslie paid his car insurance.

3  The man who paid his life insurance in December also paid his house insurance in November.

4  Tim paid his car insurance the month before Leslie paid his house insurance, but the month after Leslie paid his life insurance.

|  | Car | | | | House | | | | Life | | | |
|---|---|---|---|---|---|---|---|---|---|---|---|---|
|  | August | September | November | December | September | October | November | December | August | September | October | December |
| Gordon | | | | | | | | | | | | |
| Henry | | | | | | | | | | | | |
| Leslie | | | | | | | | | | | | |
| Tim | | | | | | | | | | | | |
| Life August | | | | | | | | | | | | |
| Life September | | | | | | | | | | | | |
| Life October | | | | | | | | | | | | |
| Life December | | | | | | | | | | | | |
| House September | | | | | | | | | | | | |
| House October | | | | | | | | | | | | |
| House November | | | | | | | | | | | | |
| House December | | | | | | | | | | | | |

| Name | Car | House | Life |
|---|---|---|---|
|  |  |  |  |
|  |  |  |  |
|  |  |  |  |
|  |  |  |  |

# Split Personalities

In a fit of resentment at her poor school report, Joanna cut photographs of five of her teachers into three pieces (head, body and legs), and then reassembled them in such a way that each "new" photograph contains pieces of three "old" ones. How have the photographs been reassembled?

1 Miss Brown's head is now in the same picture as Mr Neame's legs, but not Mr Ward's body.

2 Mr Neame's body is now topped by Mrs Moor's head.

3 Mrs Fitt's body now has Mr Ward's head, but not Miss Brown's legs.

4 Miss Brown's body isn't in the same photograph as Mrs Fitt's head or Mrs Fitt's legs.

|  |  | Body | | | | | Legs | | | | |
| --- | --- | --- | --- | --- | --- | --- | --- | --- | --- | --- | --- |
|  |  | Miss Brown | Mrs Fitt | Mrs Moor | Mr Neame | Mr Ward | Miss Brown | Mrs Fitt | Mrs Moor | Mr Neame | Mr Ward |
| Head | Miss Brown |  |  |  |  |  |  |  |  |  |  |
|  | Mrs Fitt |  |  |  |  |  |  |  |  |  |  |
|  | Mrs Moor |  |  |  |  |  |  |  |  |  |  |
|  | Mr Neame |  |  |  |  |  |  |  |  |  |  |  |
|  | Mr Ward |  |  |  |  |  |  |  |  |  |  |
| Legs | Miss Brown |  |  |  |  |  |  |  |  |  |  |
|  | Mrs Fitt |  |  |  |  |  |  |  |  |  |  |
|  | Mrs Moor |  |  |  |  |  |  |  |  |  |  |
|  | Mr Neame |  |  |  |  |  |  |  |  |  |  |
|  | Mr Ward |  |  |  |  |  |  |  |  |  |  |

| Head | Body | Legs |
| --- | --- | --- |
|  |  |  |
|  |  |  |
|  |  |  |
|  |  |  |
|  |  |  |

# The Halloween Party

The first five guests to arrive at Hal's Halloween party came in costume. Can you discover the order and costume in which each arrived?

1 Neil dressed as Frankenstein's monster and arrived earlier than the vampire, but immediately after Tanya.

2 Moira dressed as a witch and arrived earlier than James, but later than the man guest swathed in bandages in order to look like an Egyptian mummy.

3 Callum wasn't the first guest to arrive at Hal's Halloween party.

|  | Order | | | | | Costume | | | | |
|---|---|---|---|---|---|---|---|---|---|---|
|  | First | Second | Third | Fourth | Fifth | Ghost | Monster | Mummy | Vampire | Witch |
| Callum |  |  |  |  |  |  |  |  |  |  |
| James |  |  |  |  |  |  |  |  |  |  |
| Moira |  |  |  |  |  |  |  |  |  |  |
| Neil |  |  |  |  |  |  |  |  |  |  |
| Tanya |  |  |  |  |  |  |  |  |  |  |
| Ghost |  |  |  |  |  |  |  |  |  |  |
| Monster |  |  |  |  |  |  |  |  |  |  |
| Mummy |  |  |  |  |  |  |  |  |  |  |
| Vampire |  |  |  |  |  |  |  |  |  |  |
| Witch |  |  |  |  |  |  |  |  |  |  |

| Guest | Order | Costume |
|---|---|---|
|  |  |  |
|  |  |  |
|  |  |  |
|  |  |  |
|  |  |  |

# Young Farmers

Four little boys have model farms, and each farm has various numbers of cows, pigs, and sheep. How many of each type of toy animal does every boy possess?

1 The boy with three pigs has more sheep than the boy with nine cows.

2 The boy with the most sheep has one more cow than the number of pigs on his farm.

3 The tallest of the four boys has more pigs than Larry.

4 Larry has more cows than Andrew, but fewer cows than Malcolm.

5 Malcolm has fewer sheep than Andrew, who has more pigs than Malcolm.

6 Trevor has fewer than nine pigs.

|  | Cows | | | | Pigs | | | | Sheep | | | |
|---|---|---|---|---|---|---|---|---|---|---|---|---|
|  | 6 | 7 | 9 | 10 | 3 | 5 | 7 | 9 | 8 | 10 | 12 | 14 |
| Andrew |  |  |  |  |  |  |  |  |  |  |  |  |
| Larry |  |  |  |  |  |  |  |  |  |  |  |  |
| Malcolm |  |  |  |  |  |  |  |  |  |  |  |  |
| Trevor |  |  |  |  |  |  |  |  |  |  |  |  |
| Sheep 8 |  |  |  |  |  |  |  |  |  |  |  |  |
| Sheep 10 |  |  |  |  |  |  |  |  |  |  |  |  |
| Sheep 12 |  |  |  |  |  |  |  |  |  |  |  |  |
| Sheep 14 |  |  |  |  |  |  |  |  |  |  |  |  |
| Pigs 3 |  |  |  |  |  |  |  |  |  |  |  |  |
| Pigs 5 |  |  |  |  |  |  |  |  |  |  |  |  |
| Pigs 7 |  |  |  |  |  |  |  |  |  |  |  |  |
| Pigs 9 |  |  |  |  |  |  |  |  |  |  |  |  |

| Boy | Cows | Pigs | Sheep |
|---|---|---|---|
|  |  |  |  |
|  |  |  |  |
|  |  |  |  |
|  |  |  |  |

# Poster Display

Carrie has four posters on her bedroom wall, showing film stars in a scene from one of their movies. Can you discover the star featured on each poster, the title of the movie in which he plays the lead role, and the month last year in which Carrie bought the poster?

1 Poster B was bought later in the year than the one featuring James Day. Liam Foster's picture is next to and right of the one bought in May.

2 Tommy Wayne features on a poster further left than that showing a scene from *A Long Road*, which isn't furthest right.

3 The poster of Tommy Wayne was purchased earlier in the year than the one showing a scene from *Good Intentions*.

4 The still from *Way Out* is either next to and left of the poster bought in January, or it is further right than the picture of Mike Poole, not both.

5 Poster A was bought later in the year than that of a scene from *Shivers*. Poster D wasn't bought in January.

|  | Star | | | | Film | | | | Month | | | |
|---|---|---|---|---|---|---|---|---|---|---|---|---|
|  | James Day | Liam Foster | Mike Poole | Tommy Wayne | A Long Road | Good Intentions | Shivers | Way Out | January | April | May | July |
| Poster A |  |  |  |  |  |  |  |  |  |  |  |  |
| Poster B |  |  |  |  |  |  |  |  |  |  |  |  |
| Poster C |  |  |  |  |  |  |  |  |  |  |  |  |
| Poster D |  |  |  |  |  |  |  |  |  |  |  |  |
| January |  |  |  |  |  |  |  |  |
| April |  |  |  |  |  |  |  |  |
| May |  |  |  |  |  |  |  |  |
| July |  |  |  |  |  |  |  |  |
| A Long Road |  |  |  |  |
| Good Intentions |  |  |  |  |
| Shivers |  |  |  |  |
| Way Out |  |  |  |  |

**LEFT** ⇦        **RIGHT** ⇨

| A | B | C | D |

| Poster | Star | Film | Month |
|---|---|---|---|
|  |  |  |  |
|  |  |  |  |
|  |  |  |  |
|  |  |  |  |

# Fun at the Funfair

When they visited the funfair last week, the five children in this puzzle all enjoyed themselves, and each had multiple turns on the ride he or she liked best. What was each child's preference and how many times did he or she take the ride?

1 The child who thought the merry-go-round the best feature of the funfair had two more turns on the ride than George took on his preference, but one fewer turn than the child who loved the excitement of the bumper cars.

2 Helen went on her ride three more times than Olga went on the one she likes best.

3 Bill thought the ferris wheel was the fair's best feature. He went on the ride one more time than the child who preferred the swinging pirate boat.

|  | Liked | | | | | Times | | | | |
|---|---|---|---|---|---|---|---|---|---|---|
|  | Big dipper | Bumper cars | Ferris wheel | Merry-go-round | Pirate boat | 3 | 4 | 5 | 6 | 7 |
| Bill |  |  |  |  |  |  |  |  |  |  |
| Clara |  |  |  |  |  |  |  |  |  |  |
| George |  |  |  |  |  |  |  |  |  |  |
| Helen |  |  |  |  |  |  |  |  |  |  |
| Olga |  |  |  |  |  |  |  |  |  |  |
| 3 times |  |  |  |  |  |
| 4 times |  |  |  |  |  |
| 5 times |  |  |  |  |  |
| 6 times |  |  |  |  |  |
| 7 times |  |  |  |  |  |

| Rider | Liked | Times |
|---|---|---|
|  |  |  |
|  |  |  |
|  |  |  |
|  |  |  |
|  |  |  |

# Solutions

## 1

Miss Ambridge was Head Girl in 2004/05 (clue 4). Davina was Head Girl in 2002/03 (clue 2), Miss Woods in 2003/04 and Miss Mickel in 2005/06. Elaine's last name is Dale (3), so Davina's is (by elimination) Palmer and (1) Clarice served in 2005/06, thus Elaine in 2006/07. Head Girl in 2003/04 wasn't Marian (4), so Venetia, and Marian is Miss Ambridge.
**Thus:**
2002/2003 - Davina - Palmer;
2003/2004 - Venetia - Woods;
2004/2005 - Marian - Ambridge;
2005/2006 - Clarice - Mickel;
2006/2007 - Elaine - Dale.

## 2

The aunt's present wasn't bought first or second (clue 1) or fifth (clue 2), so third or fourth. Thus the castanets were bought either first or second (1). If the cigar box was bought second, then (4) the red wine was bought first, leaving no place for the castanets (above); so the cigar box for Liam's brother (4) wasn't bought second. The second gift wasn't for Liam's cousin (2) or mother (3), so his father. The first wasn't for his cousin (2) or brother (4), so his mother and (3) the sombrero was bought second. Thus the castanets were bought first (1). The sherry isn't for Liam's aunt (1), so cousin, and the red wine is for his aunt. The third purchase wasn't bought for his cousin (2), so (4) the red wine was bought third and the cigar box fourth. The sherry was thus bought fifth.
**Thus:**
Castanets - first - mother;
Cigar box - fourth - brother;
Red wine - third - aunt;
Sherry - fifth - cousin;
Sombrero - second - father.

## 3

The sum of $20 wasn't given to the charity working with the elderly (clue 1), animals (clue 2) or famine (3), so the one working with children. It wasn't given on Wednesday (1) and no donation was made on Tuesday (grid), so the children's charity received a donation on Thursday (3) and that for famine relief received Friday's donation. Wednesday's donation wasn't given to the charity for the elderly (1), so to that for animals and the donation to the charity for the elderly was made on Monday. The $35 donation wasn't made to the charity for the elderly (1) or animals (2), so famine relief. Thus Wednesday's donation wasn't of $25 (1), so $30, and $25 was given on Monday. Lou gave $20 (1) and Chris gave $35 (2). Annie gave $25 (2), so Tony gave $30.

**Thus:**
Annie - $25 - Monday - elderly;
Chris - $35 - Friday - famine;
Lou - $20 - Thursday - children;
Tony - $30 - Wednesday - animals.

## 4

The last name of the woman married in October isn't Danish (clue 2), Matthews (clue 4) or Court (5), so Unwin. The last name of the woman married in July isn't Court or Matthews (3), so Danish. Edith didn't marry three months after Mrs Danish (2), so isn't Mrs Unwin. Nor is she Mrs Danish (2) or Mrs Court (5), so Edith is Mrs Matthews. Julia isn't Mrs Court and didn't marry in July (3), so isn't Mrs Danish. Thus Julia is Mrs Unwin (who married three months after Mrs Danish, above). In clue 4, Julia is the granddaughter married to Andrew. Roger's wife isn't Edith (2), so his last name isn't Matthews. Roger's last name isn't Danish (2), so Court. The man married in July isn't Roger or Philip (3), so Bobby and (by elimination) Philip is Mr Matthews. Bobby's wife isn't Denise (1), so Stephanie. Edith's husband isn't Roger (2), so Philip, and Denise's is Roger. Denise wasn't married in January (1), so April, and Edith married in January.
**Thus:**
Denise - Roger - Court - April;
Edith - Philip - Matthews - January;
Julia - Andrew - Unwin - October;
Stephanie - Bobby - Danish - July.

## 5

Mrs Fletcher's dog wasn't awarded third or fifth prize (clue 3), nor first or second prize (clue 4), so fourth and Mrs Morris' dog achieved either first or second prize. Sam was awarded fifth prize (3). Mrs Fletcher doesn't own Butch (4), so Sam doesn't belong to Miss Barnes (1). Mr Allen's dog wasn't fifth (2), so isn't Sam. Thus Sam belongs to Mr Yates and (5) Fido was awarded third prize. Butch's owner isn't Miss Barnes (1) or Mrs Morris (4), so Mr Allen. By elimination, Fido belongs to Miss Barnes. Mr Allen's dog (Butch, above) was awarded second (1) and (2) and Nero was awarded fourth prize (Mrs Fletcher, above), so Chester was awarded first prize. Chester belongs to Mrs Morris.
**Thus:**
First prize - Chester - Mrs Morris;
Second prize - Butch - Mr Allen;
Third prize - Fido - Miss Barnes;
Fourth prize - Nero - Mrs Fletcher;
Fifth prize - Sam - Mr Yates.

## 6

The boy who washed windows bought a ship (clue 2), Harry did the dishes and Ewan did the vacuuming (clue 3). The boy who did the dusting bought a car (4), so Douglas who bought a helicopter (1) did

# Solutions

the gardening. Harry didn't buy a kite (3), so Harry bought a spinning top and Ewan bought the kite. The boy who did the windows isn't Grant (2), so Lenny. Grant thus did the dusting.

**Thus:**

Douglas - gardening - helicopter;
Ewan - vacuuming - kite;
Grant - dusting - car;
Harry - dishes - spinning top;
Lenny - windows - ship.


## 7

Dress C is white (clue 2). Dress A (furthest left) isn't red (clue 1) or beige (3), so black, thus (4) costs $3,000. The Delacci costs less than the one immediately next to and left of the red dress (1), thus the red dress isn't B, so D, and B is beige. Ducanno's is thus A (3). Delacci's isn't the red dress (D, above) or the one immediately next to and left of the red dress (C). So Delacci's is B. Dovetti's is D (2) and Delacci's is $3,250. C was thus designed by Dyablo. It isn't $4,000 (5), so $3,500. Dress D is $4,000.

**Thus:**

Dress A - Ducanno - black - $3,000;
Dress B - Delacci - beige - $3,250;
Dress C - Dyablo - white - $3,500;
Dress D - Dovetti - red - $4,000.


## 8

The tanker's hull is blue (clue 2) and the liner's is white (clue 3), so the freighter's is black (1) and the tug's is green. The tug was registered in Panama City (5). The tanker wasn't registered in Monrovia or London (2), so Hamburg. Thus it's the *Trivorn* (4). The *Carolyn* was registered in London (2) and isn't the freighter or tug (1), so the liner. By elimination, the freighter was registered in Monrovia. The tug is the *Hotari* (5) and the freighter is the *Barbel*.

**Thus:**

*Barbel* - freighter - Monrovia - black;
*Carolyn* - liner - London - white;
*Hotari* - tug - Panama City - green;
*Trivorn* - tanker - Hamburg - blue.


## 9

David ate apple pie (clue 5), so (clue 1) the MAN who ate chicken pie and pavlova is Timothy. Sarah ate beef curry (4), so (2) the venison and cheesecake were chosen by Fergus – Sarah didn't have tiramisu (4), so ice cream, and Rosie had tiramisu. Rosie didn't eat lasagne (3), so lamb's liver and David ate lasagne.

**Thus:**

David - lasagne - apple pie;
Fergus - venison - cheesecake;
Rosie - lamb's liver - tiramisu;
Sarah - beef curry - ice cream;
Timothy - chicken pie - pavlova.


## 10

Angela's item wasn't owned by her Aunt Maud, grandmother or mother (clue 4). The WOMAN (clue 1) who keeps her grandmother's brooch isn't Claire, so Judy. Mike's item was his father's (2), so Angela's belonged to her Uncle Pete. Bill has a teapot (5), so (by elimination) Aunt Maud's diary (3) is kept by Claire and Bill's item was his mother's. Mike's isn't a painting (2), so a watch. Angela keeps the painting.

**Thus:**

Angela - painting - Uncle Pete;
Bill - teapot - mother;
Claire - diary - Aunt Maud;
Judy - brooch - grandmother;
Mike - watch - father.


## 11

There are three adjacent mugs mentioned in clue 1, none of which is Harriet's green mug of water (clue 3), so Harriet's is a fourth mug. Harriet's mug isn't D (clue 3), so it's A and (1) B is either red or belongs to Richard. The mug of tea isn't B (2), so D, and C is white. By elimination, B contains coffee and Richard's mug is yellow. Mug B doesn't belong to Len (4) or Margaret (5), so Richard. Mug D is red (1). Margaret's mug isn't D (4), so C, and Len's is D.

**Thus:**

Mug A - Harriet - green - water;
Mug B - Richard - yellow - coffee;
Mug C - Margaret - white - milk;
Mug D - Len - red - tea.


## 12

The chest produced in 1914 isn't made of oak (clue 1), walnut (clue 3) or pine (5), so cedar. The oak chest was made in either 1900 or 1910 (1), so (4) the cedar chest isn't D. Nor is it B (2) or A (3), so C. The pine chest is B (5) and that made by L Turner is D. D isn't of oak (4), so walnut and A is of oak. Either B or D was made in 1900 (2), so A was made in 1910 (1) and (4) D in 1900. Wood & Co made the 1914 chest (1). By elimination, B was made in 1904. The walnut chest was made in 1900 (above), so (3) Forresters made the 1904 chest. Axe Bros thus made A.

**Thus:**

A - oak - Axe Bros - 1910;
B - pine - Forresters - 1904;
C - cedar - Wood & Co - 1914;
D - walnut - L Turner - 1900.


## 13

Danny was Bob's partner (clue 1), Colin, who finished first (clue 2), wasn't partnered by Ian (3), Geoff (4) or Adam (5), so Henry. The fifth (last) pair didn't include Bob (1), Eddie (4) or Joe (5), so Martin. Adam's

# Solutions

partner wasn't Joe or Martin (5), so Eddie. Ian and his partner were second (3), so Ian partnered Joe. By elimination, Martin's partner was Geoff. Bob and Danny weren't third (1), so fourth. Eddie and Adam were third.

**Thus:**
Bob - Danny - fourth;
Colin - Henry - first;
Eddie - Adam - third;
Joe - Ian - second;
Martin - Geoff - fifth.

## 14

Dolly who lost 20 lbs wasn't 230 lbs at the start (clue 3), so isn't 210 lbs today – nor is she 200 lbs today, so she wasn't 220 lbs at the start. Thus she started at 225 lbs and is now 205 lbs (clue 3) and Polly started at 230 lbs and is now either 200 lbs or 203 lbs. The woman who used to weigh 215 lbs now weighs 208 lbs (clue 4). The one who now weighs 210 lbs didn't start at 210 lbs (1), so 220 lbs. She isn't Holly (2) or Molly (5), so Lolly. Lolly is thus the only one to have lost 10 lbs (6), so the woman who now weighs 200 lbs started at 230 lbs (Polly, above). Molly isn't 203 lbs today (5) so 208 lbs, thus Holly was 210 lbs and is now 203 lbs.

**Thus (start - today):**
Dolly - 225 lbs - 205 lbs;
Holly - 210 lbs - 203 lbs;
Lolly - 220 lbs - 210 lbs;
Molly - 215 lbs - 208 lbs;
Polly - 230 lbs - 200 lbs.

## 15

The 8-year-old's birthday isn't on Thursday or Friday (clue 1) or Wednesday (clue 2), so Tuesday. Joanne's is on Wednesday (1) and the girl whose birthday is on Thursday will get the poster. The 7-year-old who will get slippers (3) hasn't a birthday on Tuesday or Friday, so Wednesday. Polly's birthday is on Tuesday (3). Mary isn't 6 (4), so 9 and (by elimination) Susan is 6. Mary will get a book (2), so Susan will get the poster (1) and Polly the video, Susan's birthday is on Thursday (1), so Mary's is on Friday.

**Thus:**
Joanne - slippers - Wednesday - 7;
Mary - book - Friday - 9;
Polly - video - Tuesday - 8;
Susan - poster - Thursday - 6.

## 16

Max's last name is Dawkins (clue 1). Xandra's isn't Fischer or Maine (clue 3), so Clark. Fischer isn't Pearl (2), so Roy, and Pearl's last name is Maine. *Summer* was painted by Xandra (3) and *Winter* by Roy (4). *Spring* isn't the work of Max (1), so Pearl painted *Spring* and Max painted *Autumn*. Roy's picture was produced in an earlier year than Pearl's

(2), so (above) is *Spring*. So (1) *Spring* was produced in 2003 and Max's *Autumn* in 2006. *Winter* was produced in 2002 (2), so *Summer* in 2005.

**Thus:**
*Spring* - Pearl - Maine - 2003;
*Summer* - Xandra - Clark - 2005;
*Autumn* - Max - Dawkins - 2006;
*Winter* - Roy - Fischer - 2002.

## 17

Remember throughout that each person received two different quantities (clue 1). The MAN who received 3 domestic and 8 personal samples (clue 2) isn't Alan or Bertie (3), so Micky. Alan received 4 personal (3) and Bertie 7 domestic samples. Kate didn't receive 4 domestic (5), so 5. Alan (4 personal, above) didn't receive 4 domestic (1), so Jenny received 4 domestic samples. Jenny received 7 personal (4) and Kate 5 domestic samples. Kate didn't receive 5 personal (1), so 6. Alan received 6 domestic samples. Bertie received 5 personal samples.

**Thus:**
Alan - 6 domestic - 4 personal;
Bertie - 7 domestic - 5 personal;
Jenny - 4 domestic - 7 personal;
Kate - 5 domestic - 6 personal;
Micky - 3 domestic - 8 personal.

## 18

The 29 (fewest) calls weren't in connection with Abba (clue 1), the Beach Boys or ZZ Top (clue 2) or the Beatles (3), so the Rolling Stones. The 29 calls weren't on Monday (4), so Tuesday (2); those relating to the Beach Boys were received on Wednesday and those relating to ZZ Top were received on Friday. Thus Monday's calls were in connection with the mention of the Beatles (3) and Thursday's with Abba. The Abba mention drew 42 calls (1), so that of the Beatles drew 50 (3). Thus 55 were received on Wednesday (5) and 37 on Friday.

**Thus:**
Monday - Beatles - 50 calls;
Tuesday - Rolling Stones - 29 calls;
Wednesday - Beach Boys - 55 calls;
Thursday - Abba - 42 calls;
Friday - ZZ Top - 37 calls.

## 19

Alice sent a card to Tammy (clue 1) and Vera sent to Naomi (clue 2). Tammy didn't send to Alice (intro), so Vera, and Naomi sent to Alice. Alice posted on 28 December (1) and Naomi on 30 December (3). The woman who posted on 29 December isn't Vera (2), so Tammy, and Vera posted on 27 December. Naomi's last name is Jones (2). Tammy's isn't Davis (1) or Wright (4), so Morgan. Since Tammy sent to Vera (above), Vera isn't Ms Wright (4). Thus Vera's last name is Davis and Alice's is Wright.

# Solutions

**Thus:**
Alice - Wright - Tammy - 28 Dec;
Naomi - Jones - Alice - 30 Dec;
Tammy - Morgan - Vera - 29 Dec;
Vera - Davis - Naomi - 27 Dec.

## 20

No-one spent $210 (grid). The $230 item wasn't the washing machine (clue 1), computer or dishwasher (clue 3), so the DVD player. The $150 item wasn't the washing machine (1), so the computer (3) and the dishwasher was $170. Thus the washing machine was $190. Theresa spent $230 (1). Brian spent $150 (2) and Katy spent $190. David spent $170 (1). Brian's wife is Zara (4) and Paul is married to Katy. David's wife is Annie.

**Thus:**
Brian - Zara - computer - $150;
David - Annie - dishwasher - $170;
Paul - Katy - washing machine - $190;
William - Theresa - DVD - $230.

## 21

The 17-year-old (oldest) student isn't Dean (clue 1), Robert (clue 3) or Elaine (4), so (2) Jeremy, and Nicole is 16 and took chicken soup. Thus Dean is 14 (1), the student who took tomato soup is 13 and the student who took potato soup is 15. Thus Robert is 15 (3) and the 17-year-old (Jeremy, above) took beef soup. By elimination, Dean took onion soup and Elaine is 13.

**Thus:**
Dean - 14 years old - onion;
Elaine - 13 years old - tomato;
Jeremy - 17 years old - beef;
Nicole - 16 years old - chicken;
Robert - 15 years old - potato.

## 22

The person who chose route 1 isn't Abigail (clue 1), Greg (clue 2), Simon or Theodore (3), so Emma. The person who got out after 17 minutes took route 2 (2) and Greg took route 3. Route 2 wasn't chosen by Abigail (1) or Theodore (3), so Simon (17 minutes, above). Thus Abigail chose route 5 (1) and Greg got out in 19 minutes. Emma got out in 15 minutes (3). By elimination, Theodore used route 4. He didn't take 16 minutes (4), so 18, and Abigail took 16 minutes.

**Thus:**
Abigail - route 5 - 16 minutes;
Emma - route 1 - 15 minutes;
Greg - route 3 - 19 minutes;
Simon - route 2 - 17 minutes;
Theodore - route 4 - 18 minutes.

## 23

Rosa's pupils brought in either 21 or 24 tubes (clue 1). MISS (female) Palmer (clue 2) whose pupils brought in 29 boxes and 14 tubes is thus Louise. Louise's pupils thus brought in 43 items, so the pupils of the teacher named Davis (3) brought in 26 boxes and 17 tubes (43 items). Rosa (whose pupils brought in either 21 or 24 tubes, above) isn't Davis; and Jim's pupils brought in fewer boxes than Joseph's (4), so Jim's last name isn't Davis. Thus Joseph is Davis. Jim's pupils didn't bring in 24 tubes (4), so 21 tubes. By elimination, Rosa's pupils brought in 24 tubes. Rosa's last name isn't Harper (1), so Mitchell, and Jim's is Harper. Jim's pupils brought in 24 boxes (1), so Rosa's pupils brought in 21 boxes.

**Thus:**
Jim - Harper - 24 boxes - 21 tubes;
Louise - Palmer - 29 boxes - 14 tubes;
Joseph - Davis - 26 boxes - 17 tubes;
Rosa - Mitchell - 21 boxes - 24 tubes.

## 24

The man who starts on Monday isn't an accountant (clue 1) or a car mechanic (clue 3), so a salesman and (2) the driver starts on Tuesday. Fred is an accountant (1). Randy isn't the driver (2) or car mechanic (3), so he's the salesman. The man who starts on Thursday had been out of work for 10 weeks (4), thus he isn't Fred (1). So Fred starts on Wednesday (1) and Geoff on Tuesday. By elimination, Dan starts on Thursday, so Geoff is the driver and Dan is the car mechanic. Geoff had been out of work for 11 weeks (1) and Fred for 9 weeks, so Randy had been out of work for 8 weeks.

**Thus:**
Dan - car mechanic - Thursday - 10 weeks;
Fred - accountant - Wednesday - 9 weeks;
Geoff - driver - Tuesday - 11 weeks;
Randy - salesman - Monday - 8 weeks.

## 25

Della isn't getting piece 3 or piece 5 (clue 3), so either Della Morgan (clue 1) will get piece 2 and Mrs Butcher will get piece 3, or Della will get piece 4 and Mrs Butcher will get piece 5. Candice isn't getting piece 3 or piece 5 (3), so she isn't Mrs Butcher. Thus MRS Butcher (female) is Beryl. Alan will get piece 2 (4), so Della will get piece 4 (1) and Mrs Butcher will get piece 5. By elimination, Candice will get piece 1 and Edward will get piece 3. Edward is Mr Sullivan (2). Candice's last name is Rousseau (2) and Alan's is Knowles.

**Thus:**
Alan - Knowles - piece 2;
Beryl - Butcher - piece 5;
Candice - Rousseau - piece 1;
Della - Morgan - piece 4;
Edward - Sullivan - piece 3.

# Solutions

## 26

No woman had a birthday on Thursday (grid). No man's birthday fell on the same day as that of his wife (intro), so the man whose birthday was on Tuesday is married to the woman whose birthday was on Wednesday (clue 1) and Bill's birthday was on Friday. By elimination, Mike's birthday was on Saturday (clue 2) and his wife Louise's was on Friday. Nancy's birthday was the day after David's (3), so the couple where the husband's birthday was on Tuesday and the wife's was on Wednesday (above) are Roger and Lynne. So Nancy's birthday was on Tuesday (3) and David's was on Monday. By elimination, Pete's birthday was on Thursday. Since David's birthday was on Monday, Kay's wasn't on Monday (intro), so Sunday, and Joy's was on Monday.

**Thus (his - hers):**
Bill and Joy - Friday - Monday;
David and Kay - Monday - Sunday;
Mike and Louise - Saturday - Friday;
Pete and Nancy - Thursday - Tuesday;
Roger and Lynne - Tuesday - Wednesday.

## 27

The last day at St John's isn't Wednesday (clue 2), so Tuesday (clue 1), Bayside's is on Wednesday and Tammy's school's on Thursday. Applewood's isn't on Friday (3), so Thursday, and Martin's school is Mount View which has its last day on Friday. Paul doesn't attend St John's (2), so Bayside, and Cathy attends St John's. The 6-year-old isn't Paul (2) or Cathy (4), so Martin (3), and Tammy is 9. Cathy is 7 (2) and Paul is 10.

**Thus:**
Cathy - 7 years old - St John's - Tuesday;
Martin - 6 years old - Mount View - Friday;
Paul - 10 years old - Bayside - Wednesday;
Tammy - 9 years old - Applewood - Thursday.

## 28

The men who ate 22 and 24 pies aren't Gus (clue 1) or Dave (clue 2), so Ferdy and/or Hal. Thus Hal ate 22 (2), so Ferdy ate 24. Since Hal's nickname was "Hungry" (2), Gus didn't eat 20 pies (1), so 18, and Dave ate 20. Dave was "Buster" (1) and chose apple. Ferdy chose peach (2). Gus didn't choose cherry (1), so Hal chose cherry and Gus chose rhubarb. Gus's nickname wasn't "Ravenous" (3), so "Greedy". Ferdy's nickname was "Ravenous".

**Thus:**
Dave - "Buster" - apple - 20 pies;
Ferdy - "Ravenous" - peach - 24 pies;
Gus - "Greedy" - rhubarb - 18 pies;
Hal - "Hungry" - cherry - 22 pies.

## 29

Laura lives at either No 1 or No 3 (clue 1). Jane also lives at either No 1 or No 3 (clue 3). The woman who lives at No 5 isn't Adele (1) or Molly (2), so Sarah. Molly lives at No 4 (2), so (1) Adele lives at No 2 and the woman who lives at No 1 is Laura. By elimination, Jane lives at No 3. Molly has blond hair (1) and Sarah's hair is silver (3). Laura has chestnut hair (4) and Jane's hair is black. Adele's hair is brown.

**Thus:**
Adele - No 2 - brown;
Jane - No 3 - black;
Laura - No 1 - chestnut;
Molly - No 4 - blond;
Sarah - No 5 - silver.

## 30

The person who saw the dentist on 31 January isn't Alicia (clue 1), Bernard, Colette or Tracey (clue 2), so Fred. The person who saw the dentist on 24 January isn't Alicia (1), Bernard or Colette (2), so Tracey. Tracey's second appointment was on either 10 or 15 February (3). Bernard's second wasn't on 5 or 10 February (3) and his first wasn't on 11 January (3). The person who saw the dentist on 11 January isn't Alicia (1), so Colette. Bernard saw the dentist on 17 January (2), so Alicia on 5 January (1) and Fred on 5 February. Thus Colette saw the dentist on 10 February (3) and Tracey on 15 February. Alicia's second appointment wasn't on 19 February (4), so 17 February. Bernard's second appointment was on 19 February.

**Thus:**
Alicia - 5 January - 17 February;
Bernard - 17 January - 19 February;
Colette - 11 January - 10 February;
Fred - 31 January - 5 February;
Tracey - 24 January - 15 February.

## 31

The daughter born in Sagittarius has a mother born in Libra (clue 4), but not a father born in Cancer (clue 1), Pisces or Aries (3), so Virgo. The daughter born in Leo is Carter (2) and isn't related to the woman born in Scorpio (1). The woman born in Scorpio hasn't a daughter born in Gemini (1), so Capricorn. Mr Brent was born in Aries (5) and the man born in Cancer has a daughter born in Gemini (1), so Mr Brent's daughter was born in Capricorn. The woman born in Libra isn't Mrs Adamson (4), so Mrs Dale. By elimination, the last name of the daughter born in Gemini is Adamson, so Mr Carter was born in Pisces. His wife wasn't born in Aquarius (6), so Taurus, and Mrs Adamson was born in Aquarius.

**Thus (husband - wife - daughter):**
Adamson - Cancer - Aquarius - Gemini;
Brent - Aries - Scorpio - Capricorn;
Carter - Pisces - Taurus - Leo;
Dale - Virgo - Libra - Sagittarius.

# Solutions

## 32

The Monday evening club doesn't start at 8.00pm (clue 3), so 7.30pm (clue 1) and the drama club at 7.00pm. Mr Willard runs the book club (2). Mr Jackson's club doesn't start at 7.00pm (2) and isn't the walking club. Thus Mr Jackson runs the camera club. Thursdays' meetings aren't of the drama club (1), book club (2) or walking club (3), so the camera club, and (2) the book club meets on Wednesday. The drama club doesn't meet on Monday (1), so Tuesday, and the walking club meets on Monday. Miss Payne doesn't run the drama club (1), so the walking club, and Mrs Hunter runs the drama club. Mr Jackson's club starts at 7.45pm (2), so Mr Willard's at 8.00pm.
**Thus:**
Mrs Hunter - drama - Tuesday - 7.00pm;
Mr Jackson - camera - Thursday - 7.45pm
Miss Payne - walking - Monday - 7.30pm;
Mr Willard - book - Wednesday - 8.00pm.

## 33

The birthday card was posted on the 15th (clue 3). The new home card sent to Raymond (clue 2) was thus posted on the 22nd and the new baby card on the 20th. The new job card wasn't posted on the 11th (1), so the 17th, and the get well card was posted on the 11th. The card to Adrian was thus posted on the 15th (1) and the one to Beatrice on the 11th. The WOMAN (2) who received the new baby card was (by elimination) Sheila, so the new job card was sent to Terence.
**Thus:**
Adrian - birthday - 15th;
Beatrice - get well - 11th;
Raymond - new home - 22nd;
Sheila - new baby - 20th;
Terence - new job - 17th.

## 34

The evening on which 17 pupils attended the Sports Club and 22 attended the Study Club (clue 2) wasn't Friday (clue 1), Tuesday (3), Monday or Thursday (4), so Wednesday, and (1) 25 attended Friday's Sports Club. So 18 attended Thursday's Sports Club (4), 15 attended Monday's Sports Club and (by elimination) 28 were at Tuesday's Sports Club. Thus there were 25 at Tuesday's Study Club (3). There were 13 at Monday's Study Club (4). There weren't 19 at Thursday's Study Club (2), so 18, and 19 pupils attended Friday's Study Club.
**Thus (Sports - Study):**
Monday - 15 pupils - 13 pupils;
Tuesday - 28 pupils - 25 pupils;
Wednesday - 17 pupils - 22 pupils;
Thursday - 18 pupils - 18 pupils;
Friday - 25 pupils - 19 pupils.

## 35

Monitor 2 doesn't show Tim Venton (clue 1), Ron Summers (clue 2) or Guy Hartley (3), so Bob Denny. Monitor 4 doesn't show Tim Venton (1) or Guy Hartley (3), so Ron Summers and (2) Bob Denny's bike is blue. The man on the silver bike is thus showing on monitor 4 (1) and Tim Venton is on monitor 3. By elimination, Guy Hartley is on monitor 1. The man on the green bike is one place behind Bob Denny (3), so Bob Denny is third (1) and Ron Summers (silver bike, above) is first. Guy Hartley is second (2), so Tim Venton is fourth. Tim Venton's bike is green (3), so Guy Hartley's is black.
**Thus:**
Monitor 1 - Guy Hartley - black - second;
Monitor 2 - Bob Denny - blue - third;
Monitor 3 - Tim Venton - green - fourth;
Monitor 4 - Ron Summers - silver - first.

## 36

The florist was visited on the 14th (clue 3), so Bella was accompanied to the caterer by Lucy (clue 2) on the 9th. Amy didn't go with her on the 5th or 19th (1 and calendar), so the 14th. The deposit left with the caterer was larger than that given to the florist (2), so she gave $150 to the florist (3), $100 to the hairdresser and $175 to the caterer. Thus the deposit of $125 was made on the 5th (4) and (by elimination) was given to the photographer. Robina accompanied Bella on the 5th (4) and Elizabeth accompanied her to the hairdresser on the 19th.
**Thus:**
5th - Robina - photographer - $125;
9th - Lucy - caterer - $175;
14th - Amy - florist - $150;
19th - Elizabeth - hairdresser - $100.

## 37

Either 21 delegates attended the *Good for Us* conference and 18 were at the *Positive Thoughts* conference (clue 1) or 18 were at the *Good for Us* conference and 15 were at the *Positive Thoughts* conference. In other words, 18 delegates attended either the *Positive Thoughts* or *Good for Us* conference. So *To the Future* was attended by 20 (clue 3) and 18 came from France. Thus there were 21 at the conference entitled *A New Direction* (4) and 16 came from Norway. So 18 attended the *Good for Us* conference (1) and 15 were at the *Positive Thoughts* conference. By elimination, 16 were at *The Way Forward*, so (2) 15 were from Austria. The *To the Future* delegates weren't from Sweden, so England. The delegates at *A New Direction* were from Sweden.
**Thus:**
*A New Direction* - 21 delegates - Sweden;
*Good for Us* - 18 delegates - France;
*Positive Thoughts* - 15 delegates - Austria;
*The Way Forward* - 16 delegates - Norway;
*To the Future* - 20 delegates - England.

# Solutions

## 38

Dilly the dog (clue 2) has been with Wendy either for 12 months and the hamster has been with her for 6 months, or 18 months and the hamster has been with her for 12 months; in other words, the pet that has been with her for 12 months is either the dog or the hamster. So Wendy's canary has been with her for 6 months (clue 1) and Lola has been with her for 10 months. Thus she has had her hamster for 12 months (2) and her dog for 18 months. The canary (6 months, above) isn't Bobby (1) or Kandy (3), so Midge. The rabbit has been with Wendy for 10 months (3), so the cat for 16 months. The cat isn't Kandy (4), so Bobby, and Kandy is a hamster.

**Thus:**
Bobby - cat - 16 months;
Dilly - dog - 18 months;
Kandy - hamster - 12 months;
Lola - rabbit - 10 months;
Midge - canary - 6 months.

## 39

Henry's last name is Forbes (clue 2). Albert, who plays the clarinet, isn't Dexter (clue 4) or Hale (1), so Price. The person named Dexter isn't Florence (4), so Sophie. Florence's last name is Hale. Her preference isn't Debussy (1), Elgar or Mahler (3), so Wagner. She doesn't play the oboe (1) or viola (3), so piano. The viola player prefers Elgar (3). The oboe player doesn't prefer Debussy (1), so Mahler. Thus Albert prefers Debussy. Henry doesn't play the oboe (2), so viola, and Sophie plays the oboe.

**Thus:**
Albert - Price - clarinet - Debussy;
Florence - Hale - piano - Wagner;
Henry - Forbes - viola - Elgar;
Sophie - Dexter - oboe - Mahler.

## 40

Mrs Nixon who chose Coffee Cream had an appointment at 2.00pm (clue 1), so the woman with the 2.45pm appointment chose Violent Violet (clue 3) and Nona's appointment was at 4.15pm. Naomi's was at 2.00pm (4) and Miss Neame's at 3.30pm. Nancy's was at 2.45pm (2) and Nerys' at 3.30pm. Nancy's last name isn't Nugent (2), so Norris, and Nona's is Nugent. Nerys is Miss Neame (above) and didn't choose Rowdy Red nail polish (4), so Perfect Pink. Nona chose Rowdy Red.

**Thus:**
Nancy - Norris - 2.45pm - Violent Violet;
Naomi - Nixon - 2.00pm - Coffee Cream;
Nerys - Neame - 3.30pm - Perfect Pink;
Nona - Nugent - 4.15pm - Rowdy Red.

## 41

Diane's babysitter charged $10 per hour (clue 2) and Thelma's charges $15 per hour (clue 4), so Chloë's charged $5 per hour (3) and the $10 per hour babysitter worked for 3 hours. Thus Diane's total bill was $30, so (4) Thelma's was $60, thus her babysitter worked for 4 hours. The babysitter who charged $7 per hour worked for 7 hours (1) and the one who charged $5 per hour worked for 5 hours; thus the babysitter who charges $8 per hour worked for 6 hours. Since 6 x $8 = $48 and 7 x $7 = $49, Gill's babysitter worked for 7 hours (5) and Rose's for 6 hours.

**Thus:**
Chloë - 5 hours - $5;
Diane - 3 hours - $10;
Gill - 7 hours - $7;
Rose - 6 hours - $8;
Thelma - 4 hours - $15.

## 42

The piece completed in December 2006 (most recent) has 4 holes (clue 1), so is D, *Anger* has 3 holes and is either piece A or piece E, and the piece completed in August 2005 has 2 holes and is either B or C. Piece D (December 2006) isn't *Jealousy* (clue 2), *Revenge* or *Fury* (3), so *Sorrow*. Thus *Jealousy* is A (2), B was completed in either August 2005 or August 2006 and *Jealousy* in either May 2005 or May 2006. If pieces A and B were both completed in 2005, there would be no available completion date for C (4). So piece A was completed in May 2006 and B in August 2006. Thus the August 2005 piece (1) is C and E was completed in May 2005. By elimination, *Anger* is E, *Revenge* is B (3) and *Fury* is C.

**Thus:**
Piece A - *Jealousy* - May 2006;
Piece B - *Revenge* - August 2006;
Piece C - *Fury* - August 2005;
Piece D - *Sorrow* - December 2006;
Piece E - *Anger* - May 2005.

## 43

Mr Grove (clue 2) is either Herb or Rowan. The customer served fourth wasn't Rowan (clue 1) or Herb (3), thus Mr Grove wasn't fourth. The customer served fourth isn't named Moor (1) or Bedding (3), so Hill, thus Hill is the last name of either Daisy or Ivy. MRS Moor (1) is also either Daisy or Ivy, so either Herb or Rowan is Bedding. Herb's last name isn't Bedding (3), so he's Mr Grove and Rowan's last name is Bedding. The customer served first isn't named Moor (1) or Grove (3), so Bedding. Herb bought roses (2). Rowan didn't buy carnations (1) or lilies (3), so asters. The customer who bought carnations isn't named Moor (1), so Hill. Thus Mrs Moor bought

144

# Solutions

lilies. She was served third (1), so Herb was served second. Ivy wasn't served third (4), so her last name is Hill and Daisy's last name is Moor.
**Thus:**
Daisy - Moor - lilies - third;
Herb - Grove - roses - second;
Ivy - Hill - carnations - fourth;
Rowan - Bedding - asters - first.

## 44

The man with 2 (fewest) children isn't Neil (clue 1), Dan (clue 2) or Mark (4), so Fred. The couple from Eastville have 4 children (3) and Debbie has 3. The couple with 5 (most) children aren't from Whitvale (1) or Middleton (2), so Colwood, and are Mark and his wife (4). Dan has 4 children (2), so Neil has 3. Thus Neil is Debbie's husband (above) and (2) they're from Middleton, so Fred is from Whitvale. Dan's wife is Sally (1) and Nerys has 2 children (2), so Heather is married to Mark.
**Thus:**
Dan - Sally - 4 - Eastville;
Fred - Nerys - 2 - Whitevale;
Mark - Heather - 5 - Colwood;
Neil - Debbie - 3 - Middleton.

## 45

House No 2 isn't The Willows (clue 2), Daleside or Rose House (clue 3), so Apple Lodge (1) and No 1 is High View. Rose House is No 3 (3). Miss Soul lives at The Willows (2) which isn't No 5, so No 4. Thus No 5 isn't Daleside and (3) is the home of Mrs Vane. Mr Upton lives at No 2 (2) and Mrs Walters at No 3. Mr Trimble lives at No 1.
**Thus:**
No 1 - High View - Mr Trimble;
No 2 - Apple Lodge - Mr Upton;
No 3 - Rose House - Mrs Walters;
No 4 - The Willows - Miss Soul;
No 5 - Daleside - Mrs Vane.

## 46

The 3½ hours job (longest) wasn't dusting or laundry (clue 1), ironing (clue 2) or vacuuming (3), so tidying. It wasn't done on Tuesday (4), so the tidying was on Monday (2), the laundry on Wednesday and the ironing on Friday. The dusting was on Tuesday (1), so the vacuuming on Thursday. The dusting didn't take 1 or 1½ hours (1), so 2 hours (4) and the ironing 3 hours. The laundry took 1 hour (1), so the vacuuming took 1½ hours.
**Thus:**
Dusting - 2 hours - Tuesday;
Ironing - 3 hours - Friday;
Laundry - 1 hour - Wednesday;
Tidying - 3½ hours - Monday;
Vacuuming - 1½ hours - Thursday.

## 47

Book D (furthest right) wasn't written by P Hubbard (clue 1), M Potter (clue 4) or J Barnes (5), so by S Willis. Book A isn't by P Hubbard (1) or J Barnes (5), so by M Potter and (4) *Summer Joy* is B. J Barnes didn't write book B (4), so C, and P Hubbard wrote B. Book D is *Jo's Sons* (5). Book A is *The Clock* (1), so C is *Forever*. B was published in 1987 (2), so (3) D (by S Willis, above) was published in 2005 and C in 1993. Thus book A was published in 1999.
**Thus:**
Book A - *The Clock* - M Potter - 1999;
Book B - *Summer Joy* - P Hubbard - 1987
Book C - *Forever* - J Barnes - 1993;
Book D - *Jo's Sons* - S Willis - 2005.

## 48

Person A (furthest left) is Doreen (clue 1) who didn't sell to Marcus. Joanne bought from person C (clue 2) and Andy bought from James (4), so Doreen's customer was Lucy. Person B sold the coffee pot (3). Andy and/or Marcus bought from either person B or person D, so C stood between (4) James and the table holder who sold the watering can. Thus person D sold the watering can, James is B and (by elimination) Marcus was the customer of D. Joanne didn't buy from Neil (2), so Martina, and Marcus bought from Neil. Martina didn't sell the mirror (5), so the toaster. Doreen sold the mirror.
**Thus:**
A - Doreen - Lucy - mirror;
B - James - Andy - coffee pot;
C - Martina - Joanne - toaster;
D - Neil - Marcus - watering can.

## 49

Christopher used purple paint (clue 2) and Daniel painted the chimpanzee (clue 3), so the boy (brother) who painted the red mongoose (1) is Rory. The boy (brother) who used green paint (2) is Daniel. Marina didn't use orange paint (4), so blue, and Amy used orange. Amy painted the giraffe (1). Marina didn't paint the aardvark (4), so the elephant. Christopher painted the aardvark.
**Thus:**
Amy - giraffe - orange;
Christopher - aardvark - purple;
Daniel - chimpanzee - green;
Marina - elephant - blue;
Rory - mongoose - red.

## 50

The country visited in 2000 isn't England (clue 1), Spain (clue 2) or Sweden (3), so Alice went to Canada in 2003 (4) and Germany in 2000. Spain was visited in 2004 (2). Photo E wasn't taken in 2003 (2) or 2004 (5). E wasn't taken in England (1) or Sweden (3), so (by elimination) wasn't taken in either 2002 or

# Solutions

2006. Thus E was taken in 2000. The 2003 picture is D (2). C was taken in 2004. The photo taken in England is A (1). The photo from Sweden was taken in 2002 (3), so the 2006 holiday was in England. Photo B was taken in Sweden.

**Thus:**

Photo A - England - 2006;

Photo B - Sweden - 2002;

Photo C - Spain - 2004;

Photo D - Canada - 2003;

Photo E - Germany - 2000.

## 51

Remember throughout the information in the intro and clue 1. The fruit in can A on the top shelf isn't cherries (clue 2), pears (clue 3) or lychees (4), so plums and (3) the pears are in can B. The fruit in B on the bottom shelf isn't pears (1), so cherries (2), and the pears are in A on the bottom shelf. The lychees are in D on the top shelf and C on the bottom shelf (4), so the cherries are in C on the top shelf and the plums are in D on the bottom shelf. On the middle shelf, the lychees aren't in C or D (1) or A (4), so B. On the middle shelf, the plums aren't in A or D (1), so C. On the middle shelf, the pears aren't in A (1), so D, and the cherries are in A.

**Thus (top - middle - bottom):**

Cherries - C - A - B;

Lychees - D - B - C;

Pears - B - D - A;

Plums - A - C - D.

## 52

The girl in the gold top went to the Texada (clue 3) and Shona went to QC (clue 4). Rachel who wore silver (4) isn't Colin's girlfriend who went to Laramie's (2), so Rachel went to the Blue Lagoon. Jackie's boyfriend is Dave (6), so they went to the Texada and Barbara went to Laramie's. Norman's girlfriend wore purple (1), so she's Shona. Barbara didn't wear gold (1), so pink. Jackie wore the gold top.

**Thus:**

Barbara - Colin - pink - Laramie's;

Jackie - Dave - gold - Texada;

Rachel - Pete - silver - Blue Lagoon;

Shona - Norman - purple - QC.

## 53

Gail has necklaces (clue 1) and Sandra has paintings (clue 2). Megan hasn't woven goods or pottery (4), so knitwear. Ariadne hasn't pottery (1), so woven goods, and the pottery belongs to Pauline. Pauline's table is No 12 and Megan's is No 16 (3), so Gail's is No 17 (1). No 10 isn't Sandra's (2), so Ariadne's, and No 11 is Sandra's

**Thus:**

Ariadne - No 10 - woven goods;

Gail - No 17 - necklaces;

Megan - No 16 - knitwear;

Pauline - No 12 - pottery;

Sandra - No 11 - paintings.

## 54

Phil was fourth (clue 4). The man who came first wasn't Carl (clue 1), Joe (2) or Marc (3), so Hal. Hal's problem wasn't with his radiator (5), so Carl wasn't second (1). Thus Carl was third (1) and the man who was second had radiator trouble. Marc was fifth (3) and Carl had a problem with his brakes. Thus Joe was second and (2) Hal had a problem with his steering. Phil (fourth) didn't have a problem with his accelerator (1), so his clutch. Marc had a problem with his accelerator.

**Thus:**

Carl - brakes - third;

Hal - steering - first;

Joe - radiator - second;

Marc - accelerator - fifth;

Phil - clutch - fourth.

## 55

The truck which is fourth (furthest back) in the line-up isn't carrying onions (clue 1), dog food (clue 2) or detergent (3), so footwear. Burt's isn't fourth (1), so isn't carrying footwear. Nor is Burt's truck carrying onions (1) or detergent (3), so dog food. Lance's is carrying detergent (3). Burt is further back in the line-up than the truck carrying onions (1), so the driver of the truck carrying onions isn't Dick (2). Thus Dick has footwear and Jeremy has onions. Lance's truck isn't fourth (3), so (1 and 2) Burt's is third and Dick's fourth. Burt is going to Foxburgh (1) and Dick to Capfield. Lance isn't going to Pitbury (3), so Baywood. Jeremy is going to Pitbury. Lance's truck is first (3) and Jeremy's is second.

**Thus:**

First - Lance - detergent - Baywood;

Second - Jeremy - onions - Pitbury;

Third - Burt - dog food - Foxburgh;

Fourth - Dick - footwear - Capfield.

## 56

Jane's last name is Jenkins (clue 2). Lucy's isn't Milton (clue 3), nor is her birthday on Thursday. Thus Lucy's last name isn't Connor (4), so Vaughn. The person named Connor has a birthday on Thursday (4), so Lucy's birthday is on Tuesday (3), the 16-year-old's is on Monday, and the person named Milton has a birthday on Wednesday. By elimination, Jane's birthday is on Monday. Thus Frank is 17 (1), Lucy is

15, and Michael's birthday is on Thursday. Frank's last name is Milton.

**Thus:**

Frank - Milton - Wednesday - 17;
Jane - Jenkins - Monday - 16;
Lucy - Vaughn - Tuesday - 15;
Michael - Connor - Thursday - 18.

## 57

Dolly lives in either house 4 or house 5 (clue 2), the person named Kingsley lives in house 3 and George lives in house 2. The person in house 1 isn't Jack (clue 1) or Ingrid (3), so Ella. The person in house 4 isn't Jack (1) or Ingrid (3), so Dolly. The person in house 5 isn't named Finch (1), Cooper (3) or Walsh (4), so Tate. The person in house 1 isn't named Finch (1) or Cooper (3), so Walsh. Since Ella lives in house 1 (above), the person named Cooper doesn't live in house 2 (5), so house 4, and the one named Finch lives in house 2. Jack lives in house 3 (1), so Ingrid lives in house 5.

**Thus:**

House 1 - Ella - Walsh;
House 2 - George - Finch;
House 3 - Jack - Kingsley;
House 4 - Dolly - Cooper;
House 5 - Ingrid - Tate.

## 58

The person who went to Canada first and Brazil second (clue 4) isn't Martin, Lynda or Joseph (clue 1) or Abigail (2), so Stuart. Joseph went to Italy second (1) and Abigail went to Ireland second (2). Lynda went to Jamaica first (1), but not Spain second (3), so France, and Martin went to Spain second. Martin went to Mauritius first (1). Abigail didn't holiday first in Israel (2), so Jordan. Joseph went to Israel first.

**Thus (first - second):**

Abigail - Jordan - Ireland;
Joseph - Israel - Italy;
Lynda - Jamaica - France;
Martin - Mauritius - Spain;
Stuart - Canada - Brazil.

## 59

Prince Paul was eloping (clue 5), so the Duc d'Auvil was the man escaping his wife who (clue 2) wasn't in compartment 7. Thus the Duc d'Auvil had compartment 6 (5) and Prince Paul was in compartment 7. The woman journeying as Kate Thomas had compartment 8 (3) and the passenger going to a secret meeting had compartment 4. Thus Kate Thomas was the alias of Lady Jones who (4) was carrying jewels. By elimination, Queen Jane used compartment 4. She didn't use the name Bill Smith or Oscar Lane (1), so was Sara Brown. The passenger in compartment 6 didn't call himself Bill Smith (6), so Oscar Lane. The one in compartment 7 used the name Bill Smith.

**Thus:**

Compartment 4 - Queen Jane - Sara Brown - secret meeting;
Compartment 6 - Duc d'Auvil - Oscar Lane - escaping wife;
Compartment 7 - Prince Paul - Bill Smith - eloping;
Compartment 8 - Lady Jones - Kate Thomas - carrying jewels.

## 60

No game lasted for 60 minutes (grid). The game lasting 40 minutes wasn't against Kevin King (clue 1), Bill Bishop (clue 2) or Raymond Rook (3), so Quentin Queen. The game lasting 90 minutes (longest) wasn't against Kevin King (1) or Raymond Rook (3), so Bill Bishop. His opponent in Calgary wasn't Kevin King or Quentin Queen (1) or Bill Bishop (2), so Raymond Rook. The Calgary game thus lasted for 70 minutes (1) and Kevin King was beaten in 50 minutes. The game against Bill Bishop netted a prize of $250 (3). Thus (4) the game against Bill Bishop was in Edmonton. The prize of $350 wasn't won in Calgary (2) or Vancouver (4), so Winnipeg. Kevin King didn't play in Vancouver (1), so Winnipeg, and Quentin Queen played in Vancouver. Keith won $550 in Calgary (2) and $450 in Vancouver.

**Thus:**

Calgary - Raymond Rook - 70 minutes - $550;
Edmonton - Bill Bishop - 90 minutes - $250;
Vancouver - Quentin Queen - 40 minutes - $450;
Winnipeg - Kevin King - 50 minutes - $350.

## 61

The two men, Donald and Luke (grid), are either Pippa's brother and/or uncle, so her cousin is female. Donald's picture is either No 1 or No 3 (clue 1), so he isn't Pippa's brother (clue 2), thus Luke is her brother and Donald is her uncle. Picture No 5 isn't of Luke or Pauline (3) or Magda (2), so Kirsty. No 2 isn't of Magda (2) or Pauline (3), so Luke. Magda's is No 1 (2), so Donald's is No 3 (1). Thus Pauline's is No 4. Magda is her mother (3). Pauline isn't Pippa's cousin (3), so her daughter, and Kirsty is her cousin.

**Thus:**

Picture 1 - Magda - mother;
Picture 2 - Luke - brother;
Picture 3 - Donald - uncle;
Picture 4 - Pauline - daughter;
Picture 5 - Kirsty - cousin.

## 62

The region in which there are 300 adults of non-working age isn't 4 or 3 (clue 1), 1 (clue 2) or 2 (3), so 5. The region in which there are 262 adults of working age and 282 of non-working age isn't 1 (2), 4 or 3 (1), so 2. The region with 282 adults of working age isn't 4 (1), 1 (2) or 3 (4), so 5. Region 4 hasn't 220 (1), so (4) 231 and (4) Region 3 has 240, thus Region

# Solutions

1 has 220. Region 4 has 141 adults of non-working age (1) and Region 3 has 131. There are 150 adults of non-working age in Region 1.

**Thus (working - non-working):**
Region 1 - 220 - 150;
Region 2 - 262 - 282;
Region 3 - 240 - 131;
Region 4 - 231 - 141;
Region 5 - 282 - 300.

## 63

The man with the king of clubs isn't Jimmy (clue 2), Liam (clue 3) or Martin (4), so Keith. The man with the 2 of clubs isn't Jimmy (2) or Martin (4), so Liam. Liam has either the 6 or 10 of diamonds (3) and either the 9 or jack of spades. The man with the 6 of spades isn't Keith or Jimmy (2), so Martin. The man with the ace of spades isn't Keith (1), so Jimmy, who (2) has the ace of clubs. Thus Martin has the 9 of clubs and (4) 10 of diamonds. By elimination, Liam has the 6 of diamonds. Keith has the jack of spades (2) and Jimmy has the queen of diamonds. By elimination, Keith has the 2 of diamonds and Liam has the 9 of spades.

**Thus (club - diamond - spade):**
Jimmy - A - Q - A;
Keith - K - 2 - J;
Liam - 2 - 6 - 9;
Martin - 9 - 10 - 6.

## 64

Sarah went to London on Thursday (clue 2). The child who went on Friday isn't Velma (clue 2) or Thomas (4), so Richard. Sarah went to the Monument (2), so the child who went to both Hyde Park and the Science Museum (1) did so on Wednesday and the London Eye was visited on Tuesday. By elimination, Richard went to the Globe Theatre, so (3) visited Buckingham Palace in the morning. Thomas's visit was on Tuesday (4), so Velma's was on Wednesday. The child who went to the Planetarium isn't Thomas (4), so Sarah. Thomas visited the Tower of London.

**Thus (morning - afternoon):**
Richard - Friday - Buckingham Palace - Globe Theatre;
Sarah - Thursday - Planetarium - Monument;
Thomas - Tuesday - Tower of London - London Eye;
Velma - Wednesday - Hyde Park - Science Museum.

## 65

Thomas visited both the beach and a stately home (clue 2). The child taken to a theme park on Monday isn't Velma (clue 3) or Richard (1), so Sarah. Velma didn't go to the art gallery (1), so to the castle. Richard went to the art gallery. No child was taken

out on Wednesday (grid), thus the child taken out on Tuesday wasn't Richard or Velma (1), so Thomas, to (2) a stately home. Velma's trip wasn't on Friday (4), so on Thursday (1) and Richard's was on Friday. Thomas's beach trip was on Saturday.

**Thus:**
Richard - art gallery - Friday;
Sarah - theme park - Monday;
Thomas - beach - Saturday;
Thomas - stately home - Tuesday;
Velma - castle - Thursday.

## 66

The woman at No 1 isn't Daphne (clue 1), Stephanie (clue 2), Penny or Lou (3), so Marie. The woman at No 2 isn't Daphne (1), Stephanie (2) or Penny (3), so Lou, and Steve lives at either No 1 or No 6. The men who live at Nos 3 and/or 4 aren't Damian (2), Steve (3) or Pete (4), so either Arthur or Martin. Thus Arthur lives at No 3 (1) and Daphne at No 4 with (above) Martin. Stephanie lives at No 6 (2), so Penny at No 3. Lou's partner isn't Pete (4), so Damian. Pete's partner isn't Stephanie (2), so Marie, and Steve's partner is Stephanie.

**Thus:**
Arthur - Penny - No 3;
Damian - Lou - No 2;
Martin - Daphne - No 4;
Pete - Marie - No 1;
Steve - Stephanie - No 6.

## 67

The Osgood child's party was on Saturday (clue 3). Wednesday's party to which 6 children were invited (clue 4) wasn't that of the child named McNeil (1) or Flinders (2), so Church. He/she isn't Joanne (1) or Wayne (5) and neither Joanne (1) nor Wayne (5) are named McNeil. Thus their last names are Flinders and/or Osgood. So McNeil is Brendan (5) and Lara's last name is Church. Brendan's party wasn't on Friday (2), so Thursday, and the Flinders child had a party on Friday. The child who invited 7 guests isn't Joanne (1) or Brendan (2), so Wayne. Brendan had 8 guests (1) and Joanne had 9. Seven were invited to Saturday's party (2), so Wayne's last name is Osgood and Joanne's is Flinders.

**Thus:**
Brendan - McNeil - Thursday - 8 guests;
Joanne - Flinders - Friday - 9 guests;
Lara - Church - Wednesday - 6 guests;
Wayne - Osgood - Saturday - 7 guests.

## 68

Brenda's sign is Aquarius (clue 2) and Anita's prediction was for a tough task. They are either Billy's mother and/or sister (grid). The person born under the sign of Pisces was predicted a day good for love (clue 1) and isn't Billy's father, so his brother. Mark's

148

# Solutions

sign is Scorpio (3), so (by elimination) he is Billy's father and Billy's brother is Micky. By elimination, Anita's sign is Aries. Mark's prediction wasn't that the day would be good for money (3), so his prediction was for a new friend. Thus Brenda's was that it would be a good day for money. Brenda isn't Billy's mother (3), so his sister. Anita is his mother.

**Thus:**
Anita - Aries - mother - tough task;
Brenda - Aquarius - sister - good for money;
Mark - Scorpio - father - new friend;
Micky - Pisces - brother - good for love.

## 69

Remember throughout that each "new" picture contains parts of three "old" pictures (intro). Tommy Tow's legs and Mandy Miles's head (clue 2) aren't with Faye Fisher's body. Dave Day's body has Faye Fisher's legs (clue 1), so Mandy Miles's head is with Eddie Ego's body. Eddie Ego's head has Mandy Miles's body (3), thus (by elimination) they're with Dave Day's legs. By elimination, Faye Fisher's head is with Tommy Tow's body and Tommy Tow's head has Dave Day's body, so Dave Day's head has Faye Fisher's body. Tommy Tow's body isn't with Eddie Ego's legs (4), so Mandy Miles's legs. Thus Faye Fisher's body has Eddie Ego's legs.

**Thus (head - body - legs):**
Dave Day - Faye Fisher - Eddie Ego;
Eddie Ego - Mandy Miles - Dave Day;
Faye Fisher - Tommy Tow - Mandy Miles;
Mandy Miles - Eddie Ego - Tommy Tow;
Tommy Tow - Dave Day - Faye Fisher.

## 70

No 3 has green drapes (clue 3), so Mr Pugh's apartment with blue drapes (clue 2) is No 2 and No 4 has beige curtains. No 4 isn't home to Mrs Morgan or Mr Venner (1), so (4) Mrs Quail, and Miss Turk lives at No 5. Thus Mrs Morgan lives at No 1 (1) and Mr Venner at No 3. No 1 has yellow drapes (4), so the drapes at No 5 are cream.

**Thus:**
No 1 - Mrs Morgan - yellow;
No 2 - Mr Pugh - blue;
No 3 - Mr Venner - green;
No 4 - Mrs Quail - beige;
No 5 - Miss Turk - cream.

## 71

Frank who isn't drinking cocoa (clue 1) is clockwise of the person with almond cake. Thus he hasn't black coffee (clockwise of the person with walnut cake, clue 2) or milk (clockwise of the one with chocolate cake, 3), so white coffee. Pauline hasn't black coffee

(2). The one with walnut cake is clockwise of Pauline (2), thus she hasn't cocoa (1), so milk. In clue 2, the one with black coffee is opposite Pauline. In clue 3, Pauline (milk, above) is opposite Stella. So Stella has black coffee. By elimination, James has cocoa and (1) is opposite Frank. James has seat 1 (4), so Frank has 3. Pauline hasn't 4 (3), so 2, and Stella has 4. Pauline has almond cake (1), Frank has walnut (2) and James has chocolate (3), so Stella has fruit cake.

**Thus:**
Seat 1 - James - chocolate - cocoa;
Seat 2 - Pauline - almond - milk;
Seat 3 - Frank - walnut - white coffee;
Seat 4 - Stella - fruit - black coffee.

## 72

The man who went to Vienna on the 19th didn't go to Ottawa on the 19th (intro), 11th (clue 2) or 17th (clue 3), so the 8th. Thus the man who went to Madrid on the 11th went to Vienna on the 15th (1) and Ottawa on the 19th. Whoever went to Ottawa on the 11th thus went to Vienna on the 4th; and whoever went to Vienna on the 11th went to Ottawa on the 17th. Will went to Madrid on the 4th (2). Jamie didn't go to Ottawa on the 17th or 19th (5), so didn't go to Vienna on the 11th or 15th. Dennis didn't go to Vienna on the 15th or 19th (4), so the man who went to Vienna on the 15th (and Ottawa on the 19th, above) is Brian. Jamie didn't go to Madrid on the 8th (4), so the 15th. By elimination, Dennis went to Madrid on the 8th, so (4) went to Vienna on the 4th. By elimination, Jamie went to Vienna on the 19th and Will went to Vienna on the 11th.

**Thus (Madrid - Ottawa - Vienna):**
Brian - 11th - 19th - 15th;
Dennis - 8th - 11th - 4th;
Jamie - 15th - 8th - 19th;
Will - 4th - 17th - 11th.

## 73

Mr Grover is a psychologist (clue 2) and Mrs Young has seat 6 (clue 3). The secretary who isn't in seat 6 (2) isn't Miss Blake or Mr Harte, so Mrs Neville. Since Mrs Young has seat 6 (3), Mrs Neville isn't in seat 5 (2). Seat 4 is unoccupied (intro), so (4) Mrs Neville is in seat 2 and Mr Harte is in seat 5. Mr Grover thus has seat 3 (2), so Miss Blake is in seat 1. The clerk has seat 1 (4). Seat 5 (next to the empty seat) isn't occupied by the engineer (1), so by the analyst, and the engineer has seat 6.

**Thus:**
Seat 1 - Miss Blake - clerk;
Seat 2 - Mrs Neville - secretary;
Seat 3 - Mr Grover - psychologist;
Seat 5 - Mr Harte - analyst;
Seat 6 - Mrs Young - engineer.

# Solutions

## 74

The family whose farm produces oranges has been resident for 15 years (clue 4). Farm E hasn't had the same family for 33 years (clue 3), so 27 years (2) and grapes have been grown by one family for 18 years. Farm E doesn't produce melons (1) or figs (3), so lemons. Farm A has been occupied for 18 years (5), so farm C produces figs (3) and farm D has been occupied for 33 years. By elimination, farm D produces melons and oranges are grown at farm B. Thus one family has been at farm C for 24 years.
**Thus:**

Farm A - grapes - 18 years;
Farm B - oranges - 15 years;
Farm C - figs - 24 years;
Farm D - melons - 33 years;
Farm E - lemons - 27 years.

## 75

The employee named Masters takes 14 minutes to get to work (clue 1), so the employee named Wilson takes 10 minutes (clue 2) and the chief cashier takes 18 minutes. Maggie whose last name is Poulter (3) takes four minutes longer than the manager. Thus she's the chief cashier and the person named Masters is the manager. By elimination, the employee named Cooke takes 22 minutes. Larry takes 22 minutes (1). The security guard isn't Larry (4) or Pippa, so Warren. He takes 10 minutes (4) and Pippa 14 minutes. By elimination, Larry is the assistant manager.
**Thus:**

Larry - Cooke - assistant manager - 22 minutes;
Maggie - Poulter - chief cashier - 18 minutes;
Pippa - Masters - manager - 14 minutes;
Warren - Wilson - security guard - 10 minutes.

## 76

Clive's car had blue stripes (clue 3) and made one fewer pit stop than the car with the checker design. The car with flames made one fewer pit stop than Michelle's (clue 1), thus Michelle's didn't have the checker design, so fork lightning. Larry's didn't have the checker design (2), so flames, and Pat's had the checker design. Pat's covered two more laps than Larry's (2), so Larry's completed 13 laps (1), Michelle's 12 laps and (2) Pat's 15 laps. Thus Clive's completed 14 laps. Larry's made one fewer pit stop than Michelle's (1) and one more pit stop than Pat's (2) which (4) didn't make 3 pit stops. Thus Larry's made 5 pit stops, Michelle's made 6 and Pat's made 4. Clive's made 3 pit stops.
**Thus (pit stops - laps):**

Clive - blue stripes - 3 - 14;
Larry - flames - 5 - 13;
Michelle - fork lightning - 6 - 12;
Pat - checkers - 4 - 15.

## 77

The customer who came in at 11.30am (5th) wasn't Mr Adams or Miss Lawson (clue 1) or Mrs Cole (clue 4), so (3) Mrs Pitt, and Miss Stone, who chose the turquoise carpet, came in at 11.00am. Thus the 11.30am sale was of the pink carpet (1), Mr Adams came in at 10.30am and Miss Lawson at 10.00am. By elimination, Mrs Cole came in at 9.30am, thus (2) bought the green carpet. Since Mr Adams was the third customer, his purchase wasn't of the lilac carpet (5), so blue, and Miss Lawson chose the lilac carpet.
**Thus:**

Mr Adams - 10.30am - blue;
Mrs Cole - 9.30am - green;
Miss Lawson - 10.00am - lilac;
Mrs Pitt - 11.30am - pink;
Miss Stone - 11.00am - turquoise.

## 78

Hazel drives car 3 (clue 3), so Jeremy owns car 4 (clue 4) and a WOMAN (thus not Alan) drives 22 miles in car 2. Alan doesn't own car 5 (2), so car 1. Thus (by elimination) he drives 17 miles (2) and the owner of car 5 drives 14 miles. If Gemima owns car No 2 (22 miles, above), then Alan's car (car 1, above) would travel three more miles than Gemima's (1). But Alan's car travels 17 miles (above). Thus Gemima owns car 5, so Tricia owns car 2. Jeremy travels 19 miles (5), so Hazel covers 25 miles.
**Thus:**

Car 1 - Alan - 17 miles;
Car 2 - Tricia - 22 miles;
Car 3 - Hazel - 25 miles;
Car 4 - Jeremy - 19 miles;
Car 5 - Gemima - 14 miles.

## 79

Debbie Dean was lead singer with Loose Ends (clue 1) and Kathy Krush performed at Ocean River (clue 3). The lead singer with Fathers' Fear who appeared at Rocky Lake wasn't Phil Potter (2), so Graham Good. Kathy Krush wasn't with the Dormice (3), so The Rave, and Phil Potter sang with The Dormice. Loose Ends didn't perform at Deep Falls (1), so Smallwood, and The Dormice were at Deep Falls. The resort in which James worked in 1986 wasn't Rocky Lake or Smallwood (2) or Ocean River (3), so Deep Falls. He was in Smallwood in 1984 (1). James worked in Rocky Lake in 1985 (2), so in Ocean River in 1983.
**Thus:**

1983 - Ocean River - The Rave - Kathy Krush;
1984 - Smallwood - Loose Ends - Debbie Dean;
1985 - Rocky Lake - Fathers' Fear - Graeme Good;
1986 - Deep Falls - The Dormice - Phil Potter.

# Solutions

## 80

Ms Moore ordered salad (clue 3) and Mr Fischer ordered whiskey and soda. The person who (clue 4) ordered both a hamburger and coffee isn't Mrs Thorn, so Mr Watson. The person in room 404 didn't order orange juice (1), whiskey and soda (3) or coffee (4), so beer. Thus the club sandwich is for room 403 (2). The person in room 401 hasn't asked for a muffin (1) or salad (3), so a hamburger, and (4) Mrs Thorn has room 402. Ms Moore has room 404 (3) and Mr Fischer has room 403, so the orange juice and muffin are for room 402.

**Thus:**
Room 401 - Mr Watson - coffee - hamburger;
Room 402 - Mrs Thorn - orange juice - muffin;
Room 403 - Mr Fischer - whiskey and soda - club sandwich;
Room 404 - Ms Moore - beer - salad.

## 81

Sonja is married to Mike (clue 5). Rachel gave birth to Philip (clue 6), whose father isn't Ray. Nor is Philip's father Roy or Peter (1), so he's Steve. Sally's husband isn't Roy (1) or Peter (5), so Ray, Peter's partner isn't Mary (3), so Pamela. Thus Roy's partner is Mary whose baby (3) is May. Joy's father isn't Peter or Mike (2), so Ray. Pamela's baby isn't Sammy (4), so Dennis. Mike's baby is Sammy.

**Thus:**
Mike - Sonja - Sammy;
Peter - Pamela - Dennis;
Ray - Sally - Joy;
Roy - Mary - May;
Steve - Rachel - Philip.

## 82

The girl at No 1 (furthest west) isn't Bella or Pamela (clue 2), Collette or Tracey (clue 4), so Nadine. The girl at No 9 (furthest east) isn't 10 (2), 12 (3), 9 or 11 (5), so she's 13 years old. She isn't Pamela or Tracey (1) or Bella (5), so Colette. The girl at No 7 isn't Pamela or Tracey (1), so Bella. The 12-year-old isn't Pamela or Tracey (1) or Nadine (3), so Bella. The 9-year-old lives further east than Tracey (6), so she isn't Nadine. Thus Pamela is 9 and lives at No 5 and Tracey lives at No 3. Nadine isn't 11 (4), so she's 10 and Tracey is 11.

**Thus:**
No 1 - Nadine - 10 years old;
No 3 - Tracey - 11 years old;
No 5 - Pamela - 9 years old;
No 7 - Bella - 12 years old;
No 9 - Colette - 13 years old.

## 83

Tuesday's interview wasn't in Appleton (clue 1), Oakfield (clue 2) or Westford (3), so Dayville. Thus his interview with Mary Kay wasn't in Dayville, Appleton or Oakfield (1), so Westford and (3) Mary Kay is the singer. Appleton was visited the day before Westford (1), so (3) Naomi Noon was in Appleton. Anni Jones is the actress (2). Naomi Noon isn't the TV producer (1), so the dancer. Anni Jones wasn't interviewed in Oakfield (2), so Dayville, and the TV producer was in Oakfield. By elimination, the TV producer is Suzi Taylor. Ivor's interview with Suzi was on Wednesday (1) and he went to Appleton on Thursday, so Westford on Friday.

**Thus:**
Tuesday - Dayville - Anni Jones - actress;
Wednesday - Oakfield - Suzi Taylor - TV producer;
Thursday - Appleton - Naomi Jones - dancer;
Friday - Westford - Mary Kay - singer.

## 84

Jim's glider is yellow (clue 3) and the white glider was brought down on the main road. Des landed on the firing range on Friday (clue 1), thus his glider isn't blue (2), so purple. The glider which came down in the safari park isn't blue (2), so yellow and the blue glider came down on the beach. Colin's mistake was on Thursday (4), thus the pilot of the blue glider made a mistake on Monday (2) and Jim's was on Tuesday. By elimination, Aidan's glider is blue and Colin's is white.

**Thus:**
Aidan - blue - Monday - beach;
Colin - white - Thursday - main road;
Des - purple - Friday - firing range;
Jim - yellow - Tuesday - safari park.

## 85

No show is on Wednesday or Saturday evenings (grid). *Laugh a Lot* is on Tuesdays (clue 2) and *Sports Slot* on Mondays (clue 4), so Simon watches *News Review* (3) on Thursdays and *World's End* is on Fridays. *Cartoon Capers* is on Sundays. Laurence watches *World's End* (1) and Jessica watches *Cartoon Capers*. The MAN who watches *Laugh a Lot* (2) is Alan. Karen watches *Sports Slot*.

**Thus:**
Alan - *Laugh a Lot* - Tuesday;
Jessica - *Cartoon Capers* - Sunday;
Karen - *Sports Slot* - Monday;
Laurence - *World's End* - Friday;
Simon - *News Review* - Thursday.

# Solutions

## 86

John lives at No 8 (clue 3). The resident at No 12 isn't Thomas (clue 1), Louise (clue 2) or Brenda (4), so Sarah. Thus the niece visited No 10. Either Louise lives at No 9 and a daughter visited No 8 (2) or Louise lives at No 10 and a daughter visited No 9. In other words, the resident at No 9 is either Louise or was visited by a daughter. Brenda's visitor was her grandson (4), so she isn't at No 9. Thomas isn't at No 9 (1), so the person at No 9 is Louise and (2) the resident at No 8 (John, above) was visited by a daughter. The niece visited No 10 (above), so Brenda is at No 6 and Thomas is at No 10. A son visited No 12 (1), so a nephew visited No 9.

**Thus:**

No 6 - Brenda - grandson;
No 8 - John - daughter;
No 9 - Louise - nephew;
No 10 - Thomas - niece;
No 12 - Sarah - son.

## 87

Mathematics was the subject of week 3's exam on Monday (clue 3), so the Tuesday exam was in week 1 and the geography exam was in week 2 (clue 2). Week 4's exam wasn't on Thursday (4), so Wednesday, and week 2's was on Thursday. Week 1's excuse was earache (2). Dizzy spells was the English exam excuse (1), so week 1's exam was in science and week 4's was in English. Week 3's excuse wasn't a knee injury (3), so stomach pains, and a knee injury was week 2's excuse.

**Thus:**

Week 1 - Tuesday - science - earache;
Week 2 - Thursday - geography - knee injury;
Week 3 - Monday - mathematics - stomach pains;
Week 4 - Wednesday - English - dizzy spells.

## 88

No-one is 40 years old (grid). The 38-year-old (youngest) isn't Patricia (clue 1), Leanne (clue 3) or Tom (4), so Charles. The 44-year-old (oldest) doesn't play the tuba (1), cello (2) or flute (4), so the violin and (3) Leanne is 42. Tom isn't three years older than Patricia (4), so Patricia isn't 41 and Tom isn't 44. Thus Tom is 41 and Patricia is 44. Charles plays the flute (4). Patricia (violinist, above) isn't directly next to Leanne (3), so (2) Leanne doesn't play the cello. Thus Tom plays the cello and Leanne the tuba. Tom is directly next to and right of Patricia (2) who is further right than but not next to Leanne (3), so Leanne is A, Patricia is C and Tom is D. B is Charles.

**Thus:**

Charles - B - flute - 38 years old;
Leanne - A - tuba - 42 years old;
Patricia - C - violin - 44 years old;
Tom - D - cello - 41 years old.

## 89

Cora won 6 games in the first set and 3 in the second set (clue 1), so Laura won 4 in the second and 7 in the first (clue 3). Flora won 5 and Nora 7 in the second set (2), so Dora won 6 in the second. Cora's total number of games was 9 and Laura was 11, so (4) Dora won 4 in the first set, Flora won 3 in the first set and Nora 5 in the first set.

**Thus (1st set - 2nd set):**

Cora - 6 - 3;
Dora - 4 - 6;
Flora - 3 - 5;
Laura - 7 - 4;
Nora - 5 - 7.

## 90

The egg bought first wasn't wrapped in orange or silver (clue 1), pink (clue 2) or gold (3), so purple foil. The egg bought fifth wasn't for Deborah (1), Samantha (2), Jasmine or Belinda (3), so Jessica. Deborah's egg wasn't in orange or silver (1) or pink (2), so gold. Thus Jasmine's was bought immediately before Deborah's (3). Jessica's (5th, above) wasn't in orange foil (4), so (1) the egg in orange was bought fourth, Deborah's third and the one in silver was bought second and (above) given to Jasmine. By elimination, Jessica's egg was in pink foil. Belinda's egg was bought first (3), so Samantha's fourth.

**Thus:**

Belinda - first - purple;
Deborah - third - gold;
Jasmine - second - silver;
Jessica - fifth - pink;
Samantha - fourth - orange.

## 91

The Taj Mahal is a gift for a wife (clue 1) and the CN Tower is for a brother (clue 4). The model made for an uncle isn't of Tower Bridge (2), so the Eiffel Tower, and Tower Bridge is for a nephew. The Eiffel Tower has 4,344 matchsticks (2), so wasn't made by Jane (1), Cliff (3) or Paul (5), so Ron. Cliff's isn't for his wife or brother (3), so nephew. Jane's isn't of the Taj Mahal (1), so the CN Tower. Thus the Taj Mahal was made by Paul for (1) his wife and Jane's model is for her brother. Jane didn't use 2,468 matchsticks (4), so 3,715 (1) and Paul used 4,022. Cliff used 2,468 matchsticks.

**Thus:**

Cliff - Tower Br - 2,468 - nephew;
Jane - CN Tower - 3,715 - brother;
Paul - Taj Mahal - 4,022 - wife;
Ron - Eiffel Tower - 4,344 - uncle.

## 92

Remember throughout that each woman visited three different shops (intro). Sue went to the grocer first

# Solutions

(clue 3) and Diane to the newsagent third (clue 1). Diane didn't go the butcher first (1), so the baker; thus Diane visited either the butcher or grocer second. So (2) Mandy went to the butcher first and Diane went to the butcher second. Mandy went to the baker third (1). By elimination, Sue went to the butcher third and Cheryl went to the grocer third. Cheryl also went to the newsagent first, so Cheryl went to the baker second, Mandy went to the grocer second and Sue went to the newsagent second.

**Thus (first - second - third):**
Cheryl - newsagent - baker - grocer;
Diane - baker - butcher - newsagent;
Mandy - butcher - grocer - baker;
Sue - grocer - newsagent - butcher.


## 93

Cuthbert's cat is Daisy (clue 1) and Marmaduke is at either No 4 or No 5 (clue 3). Chris is at either No 2 or No 3 (2) and his cat isn't Nero or Sooty, so Lucky. Caitlin lives at either No 1 or No 2 and her cat isn't Marmaduke (3). Nero isn't at No 1 or No 2 (2), so Caitlin's cat is Sooty. They don't live at No 2 (2), so No 1 and (3) Marmaduke lives at No 4. Daisy isn't at No 2 (with Chris, above). Cuthbert isn't at No 3 (1), so he and Daisy are at No 5, and Nero is at No 3. Cathy isn't at No 4 (4), so No 3. Colin lives at No 4.

**Thus:**
No 1 - Sooty - Caitlin;
No 2 - Lucky - Chris;
No 3 - Nero - Cathy;
No 4 - Marmaduke - Colin;
No 5 - Daisy - Cuthbert.


## 94

Remember throughout that no resident has a rhyming first name and last name (intro) and that there are two men and three women. The three women's names are Kate, Penny and Sue, so the men are Ray and Terry. The woman named Tate (clue 2) isn't Kate (rhyme) or Sue, so Penny. If Penny and Terry live at Nos 3 and/or 4 (clue 2), then Sue lives at No 5. But then the person named Pugh lives at No 5 (1), so Sue's last name would be Pugh, which (rhyme) isn't possible. So Penny and Terry live at either No 1 and/or No 2. Since Penny's last name is Tate (above), Terry doesn't live at No 1 (3), so he lives at No 2. Penny lives at No 1. The person named Pugh lives at No 5 (1) and Ray lives at No 4. Terry's last name isn't Perry (rhyme), so Renny, and the person named Perry lives at No 4. Sue's last name isn't Pugh (rhyme), so Day. Kate's last name is Pugh.

**Thus:**
No 1 - Penny - Tate;
No 2 - Terry - Renny;
No 3 - Sue - Day;
No 4 - Ray - Perry;
No 5 - Kate - Pugh.


## 95

Remember throughout the information given in clue 1. Piece C is orange (clue 3), so pieces H, I and K are not (1). D is yellow (4), so J and K are not (1), F is red (5), so B and E are not (1). Thus A is red and (1) G is not. By elimination, B is green, so G and I are not (1). H isn't green (2), so yellow. Thus G isn't yellow (1), so orange. L isn't orange (6), so green, and J is orange. K isn't green (1), so red. Thus E is green, so I is yellow.

**Thus (square - triangle upper - triangle lower):**
Green - B - E - L;
Orange - C - G - J;
Red - A - K - F;
Yellow - D - I - H.


## 96

The people born in June and September aren't Dougal (clues 2 and 3) or Darren (clue 4), so Dean and/or Donny. One birthday is 13th September (3), so Darren's isn't in August (4). Thus Darren's is in July and Dougal's is in August, so (4) on the 9th. The 20-year-old's isn't in July (1), so (2) Donny is 21 and Darren is 19. Dougal (9th, above) isn't 22 (4), so 20 and Dean is 22. Dean's birthday is in June (4), so Donny's is in September on (3) the 13th. Dean's is on the 15th (1), so Darren's is on the 11th.

**Thus:**
Darren - 19 - 11th - July;
Dean - 22 - 15th - June;
Donny - 21 - 13th - September;
Dougal - 20 - 9th - August.


## 97

Pot A (furthest left and the same size as B) wasn't bought on Tuesday (clue 2), Wednesday (clue 3), Thursday (4) or Friday (5), so Monday and (1) the lilies are in B. The crocuses are in either C or E (3), as are the hyacinths (5) and pots B and D were bought on either Wednesday (3) or Friday. A doesn't contain snowdrops (2), so tulips, and the snowdrops are in D. Thursday's purchase wasn't of hyacinths (4), so crocuses, and the hyacinths were bought on Tuesday. E was bought on Tuesday (2), so C contains crocuses and (3) B was bought on Wednesday. Thus D was bought on Friday.

**Thus:**
Pot A - tulips - Monday;
Pot B - lilies - Wednesday;
Pot C - crocuses - Thursday;
Pot D - snowdrops - Friday;
Pot E - hyacinths - Tuesday.


## 98

The 7-year-old (youngest) child isn't Quentin or Wendy (clue 1), Stephen or Rebecca (clue 3), so Tim. The 11-year-old (oldest) child isn't Quentin (1),

Rebecca (2) or Stephen (3), so Wendy. Quentin is either 9 or 10 (1), so doesn't own Towser (3). Towser's owner isn't Stephen or Rebecca (3) and Stephen is older than Towser's owner, who thus isn't Wendy, so Tim. Quentin isn't 9 (1), so 10, and Spot's owner is 8. Stephen is 8 (3) and Rebecca is 9. Quentin owns Benji (2). Rebecca doesn't own Bob (2), so Rolf. Wendy owns Bob.
**Thus:**
Quentin - Benji - 10 years old;
Rebecca - Rolf - 9 years old;
Stephen - Spot - 8 years old;
Tim - Towser - 7 years old;
Wendy - Bob - 11 years old.

## 99

Yacht D isn't the *Andromeda* or *Saucy Sue* (clue 1) or *Jamboree* (clue 3), so it's the *Fandango* which (2) was built in either 2002 or 2005. Thus it wasn't built two years earlier than any other yacht. So (1) the *Andromeda* is A, the *Saucy Sue* is B and the yacht built two years earlier than the *Andromeda* is C and (by elimination) is the *Jamboree*. C has a white hull (3) and D (*Fandango*, built in 2002 or 2005, above) was built two years later than the yacht with the green hull. Thus D was built in 2002 and the one with a green hull in 2000. The yacht with a blue hull was built in 2005 (2), so C was built in 1998. The *Andromeda* was built in 2000 (1), so B was built in 2005. Yacht A has a green hull (3), so D has a red hull.
**Thus:**
Yacht A - *Andromeda* - green - 2000;
Yacht B - *Saucy Sue* - blue - 2005;
Yacht C - *Jamboree* - white - 1998;
Yacht D - *Fandango* - red - 2002.

## 100

No couple married in November (grid). The couple saving for a house were married in September (clue 3), so Kathy, who is saving for a boat (clue 4) married in October, Debbie in December and Terence in either August or September. Dawn was married in September (2). The couple saving for a vacation married in December (1) and Neville married in October. By elimination, the couple married in August are saving for a car. The man married in August isn't Neville (above), so Dawn isn't married to Neil (2). Thus Terence and/or Tommy married in August and/or September (2) and Neil married in December. By elimination, Karen and her husband are saving for a car. Karen's husband isn't Tommy (5), so Terence. Dawn is married to Tommy.
**Thus:**
Neil - Debbie - December - vacation;
Neville - Kathy - October - boat;
Terence - Karen - August - car;
Tommy - Dawn - September - house.

## 101

Tina's singing position was either fourth and her dancing position was first (clue 2) or fifth and her dancing position was second. Thus Jenny's dancing position was either third or fourth (clue 1). Davina's singing position wasn't first or second (1) and Clarissa's dancing position wasn't fifth (4), so the woman placed second in singing and fifth in dancing (3) is Wyn. Clarissa was first in dancing (4), so Tina was second in dancing and (2) fifth in singing. Jenny was first in singing (1) and Davina was third, so Clarissa was fourth. Jenny was fourth in dancing (1), so Davina was third.
**Thus (singing - dancing):**
Clarissa - fourth - first;
Davina - third - third;
Jenny - first - fourth;
Tina - fifth - second;
Wyn - second - fifth.

## 102

The men who ate 30 and 32 cookies aren't Jack (clue 1) or Keith (clue 2), so Lee ate 30 (3) and Martin ate 32. Lee didn't eat 25 candies (1), so the man who ate 25 candies ate 24 cookies (2) and Keith ate 20 cookies. The man who ate 26 cookies isn't Jack (1), so Noel, and Jack ate 24. Lee ate 24 candies (1). Keith ate 20 candies (4), Martin ate 23 and Noel ate 19 candies.
**Thus:**
Jack - 25 candies - 24 cookies;
Keith - 20 candies - 20 cookies;
Lee - 24 candies - 30 cookies;
Martin - 23 candies - 32 cookies;
Noel - 19 candies - 26 cookies.

## 103

Charlotte returned on the 25th (clue 1), so (only possibility) started her visit on the 18th and stayed for 7 days. She didn't stay with an aunt (clue 1), so someone stayed with an aunt for 9 days (2) and the person whose visit to a friend started on the 11th stayed for 11 days. Jessica thus went on the 6th and stayed for 5 days (3) and Victor went on the 2nd and stayed for 9 days (aunt, above). By elimination, Norman went on the 11th, thus (2) he visited a friend. Jessica didn't visit her grandfather (3), so her cousin. Charlotte visited her grandfather.
**Thus:**
Charlotte - grandfather - 18th - 7 days;
Jessica - cousin - 6th - 5 days;
Norman - friend - 11th - 11 days;
Victor - aunt - 2nd - 9 days.

## 104

The dog aged 15 months (youngest) doesn't belong to Mr Cheeseman (clue 2), Mrs Lester (clue 3) or Mr Gray (4), so to Mrs Turton. It didn't come first (1), so

# Solutions

Mr Gray's dog isn't 18 months old (4). The 18-month-old dog doesn't belong to Mr Cheeseman (2), so to Mrs Lester. So Cleo belongs to Mrs Turton and wasn't fourth (3). Max is Mr Cheeseman's dog and is either 22 or 25 months old (2) and the dog in second place is either 15 or 18 months old. Cleo (youngest, above) wasn't first (1), so Mrs Lester's dog wasn't first or second (3). Thus Cleo was second (2 and 3) and Mr Cheeseman's dog is 22 months old. Mr Gray's is thus 25 months old. It didn't finish in first place (4), so Max came first. Thus Tim belongs to Mr Gray (1), so Mrs Lester's dog is Glen. Glen wasn't fourth (5), so third and Tim was fourth.

**Thus:**
Cleo - Mrs Turton - 15 months old - second;
Glen - Mrs Lester - 18 months old - third;
Max - Mr Cheeseman - 22 months old - first;
Tim - Mr Gray - 25 months old - fourth.

## 105

Section 10 won't be used for beans (clue 1), onions (clue 2), lettuce (3) or carrots (4), so potatoes. The potatoes to the west won't be in sections 1 or 3 (clues 2 and 3) 5 or 9 (3), so 7, and neither the onions (2) nor lettuce (3) will be in section 8. Section 1 won't be used for beans (1), carrots (2) or onions (4), so lettuce. Onions won't be in sections 5 or 9 (4), so 3, and carrots will be in section 2. By elimination, beans will be in section 8, so (1) also in 9. Carrots will thus be in section 5. Onions will be in section 4 (2), so lettuce will be in section 6.

**Thus (west - east):**
Beans - 9 - 8;
Carrots - 5 - 2;
Lettuce - 1 - 6;
Onions - 3 - 4;
Potatoes - 7 - 10.

## 106

Either the man from Manitoba has a personal best of 300 yards and the man from Nova Scotia has a personal best of 280 yards (clue 1) or the man from Manitoba has a personal best of 320 yards and the man from Nova Scotia has a personal best of 300 yards. In other words, the man with a personal best of 300 yards is from either Manitoba or Nova Scotia. So the man from Quebec has a personal best of 290 yards (clue 2) and Frank's is 320 yards. Albert from Ontario (3) has (by elimination) a personal best of 330 yards and Frank is thus from Alberta (3). So the personal best of the man from Manitoba is 300 yards (1) and that of the man from Nova Scotia is 280 yards. Larry's personal best is 300 yards (4) and Neil's is 280 yards. Thus James is representing Quebec.

**Thus:**
Albert - Ontario - 330 yards;
Frank - Alberta - 320 yards;
James - Quebec - 290 yards;
Larry - Manitoba - 300 yards;
Neil - Nova Scotia - 280 yards.

## 107

Remember throughout that there are three different quantities of suns, moons and stars in each picture (intro). Thus the picture with 4 suns has either 3 or 7 stars (clue 1) and the picture with 5 stars has either 6 or 7 moons (clue 3). The picture with 4 moons hasn't 6 stars (1) or 7 stars (2), so 3 stars. The picture with 4 moons isn't C (2), so (3) C has 3 moons. The picture with 4 moons and (above) 3 stars hasn't 4 or 3 suns (intro), so (by elimination) the picture with 4 suns has 7 stars and (1) the picture with 6 stars has 7 moons. By elimination, the picture with 4 suns has 3 moons and (3) the one with 5 stars has 6 moons. Picture B has 5 suns (2) and picture A has 4 moons (and 3 stars, above). Picture A hasn't 3 or 4 suns (intro), so 7 suns, and D has 3 suns. Picture B (5 suns, above) hasn't 5 stars (intro), so 6 (and 7 moons, above). Picture C has 4 suns. Picture D has 6 moons and 5 stars.

**Thus (suns - moons - stars):**
Picture A - 7 - 4 - 3;
Picture B - 5 - 7 - 6;
Picture C - 4 - 3 - 7;
Picture D - 3 - 6 - 5.

## 108

The item bought fourth wasn't the bed (clue 1), drapes (clue 2) or freezer (4), so the table. It wasn't sold by Peter (1), Stan (3) or Angela (freezer, 4), so Geraldine, and (3) Stan was at the third store visited. Angela sold the freezer (4). The bed wasn't sold by Peter (1), so Stan, and Peter sold the drapes. Shop Rite was visited fourth (1). Stan doesn't work at Lo Cost (3) or Wize Buys (5), so Downton's, and (2) the drapes were bought second. By elimination, the freezer was bought first. Angela doesn't work at Wize Buys (5), so Lo Cost. Peter works at Wize Buys.

**Thus:**
Downton's - third - Stan - bed;
Lo Cost - first - Angela - freezer;
Shop Rite - fourth - Geraldine - table;
Wize Buys - second - Peter - drapes.

## 109

Whoever skied in France is now in Spain (clue 2). The person now in Canada didn't ski in Canada (clue 1), Scotland (3) or Italy (4), so Switzerland. The person now in Scotland didn't ski in Scotland (1) or Canada (3), so Italy and (4) is Jodi. Toby didn't ski in Scotland (4), so Switzerland (5) and William skied in Scotland. Kevin is now in France (2), so (by elimination) Marcia

is in Spain and William is in Norway. Kevin didn't ski in France (1), so Canada. Marcia skied in France.
**Thus (skied in - now in):**
Jodi - Italy - Scotland;
Kevin - Canada - France;
Marcia - France - Spain;
Toby - Switzerland - Canada;
William - Scotland - Norway.

## 110

Gayle hid under a bush (clue 3). The child who hid behind a rock wasn't Fiona or Sally (clue 1) or Robert (3), so Benjamin. He didn't take 6 minutes to find (1), so 5 (4) and Sally was found after 2 minutes. Fiona took 6 minutes to find (1). Sally wasn't up a tree (2) or behind a tree (3), so in a shed and (2) the child up the tree took 4 minutes to find. By elimination, Gayle took 3 minutes to find, so Robert was found in 4 minutes and Fiona hid behind a tree.
**Thus:**
Benjamin - behind a rock - 5 minutes;
Fiona - behind a tree - 6 minutes;
Gayle - under a bush - 3 minutes;
Robert - up a tree - 4 minutes;
Sally - in a shed - 2 minutes.

## 111

The man who played the part of Pete Prior in 2003 isn't Neil (clue 2), Frank or Graham (clue 3), so Alan, whose last name is Bourne (1). No movie was released in 2004 (grid), so Mr Montgomery played the part in 2005 (2) and Neil in 2007. Frank is thus Mr Montgomery (3), so Graham played the part in the 2006 movie. Graham's last name isn't Fontaine (3), so Steele and Neil's is Fontaine. Alan starred in the 2003 movie (above), so *Dead Ringer* was released in 2005 (1) and *Forget Her* in 2007. Graham (Steele, above) didn't appear in *His Final Word* (4), so *Cold Case*. Thus Alan Bourne was in *His Final Word*.
**Thus:**
*Cold Case* - Graham - Steele - 2006;
*Dead Ringer* - Frank - Montgomery - 2005;
*Forget Her* - Neil - Fontaine - 2007;
*His Final Word* - Alan - Bourne - 2003.

## 112

The person who spent $30 on wine isn't Lisa (clue 2), Tony (clue 3) or Annabel (4), so Scott. No-one spent $40 on wine (grid), so the person named Barber spent $38 (5). The one who spent $48 on wine isn't named Harper (2) or Taylor (3), so Samson. Lisa isn't Samson (1), so the person who spent $42 on wine isn't named Harper (2), thus Taylor spent $42 and Harper spent $30 on wine. Tony spent $48 on wine (3), so his last name is Samson (above). Scott's last name is Harper (above). Tony spent $5 more than Lisa on beer (1) and he spent more than Scott on beer (2). Since he spent $48 on wine (above), he isn't

the person who spent $35 on beer (4), so he spent $40 on beer and (1) Lisa spent $35. Thus Lisa spent $38 on wine (4) and Annabel spent $42. Lisa is thus Barber (above), so Scott didn't spent $30 on beer (6). Thus Scott spent $25 and Annabel spent $30 on beer.
**Thus (beer - wine):**
Annabel - Taylor - $30 - $42;
Lisa - Barber - $35 - $38;
Scott - Harper - $25 - $30;
Tony - Samson - $40 - $48.

## 113

Bruce has more in his vacation piggy bank than Victoria (clue 3), so he isn't the child with $13 in the day-to-day box (clue 1). The child with $13 isn't Kenny or Victoria (1) and no child has $14 (grid), so Stephen hasn't $13 (2), thus Patricia has $13 and Stephen has $12. Patricia hasn't $22 in her vacation box (1), and no child has $25. Patricia has less in her vacation box than Victoria (1) and Victoria has less in her vacation box than Bruce (3), so Patricia hasn't $26. Thus Patricia has $23 and Stephen $24 (2). Victoria has $26 and Bruce $27 (3), so Kenny has $22. Victoria doesn't have $16 in her day-to-day box (3). If she has $15, then her combined total is $41, so Kenny's would be $42 (4) which, since he has $22 in his vacation piggy bank but can't have $20 in his day-to-day box, is impossible (grid), thus Victoria has $10 (total $36) and Kenny has $15. Bruce has $16.
**Thus (day-to-day - vacation):**
Bruce - $16 - $27;
Kenny - $15 - $22;
Patricia - $13 - £23;
Stephen - $12 - $24;
Victoria - $10 - $26.

## 114

The kitchen will be cream (clue 3). The bathroom won't be lemon or lime (clue 2) or white (4), so pale blue. The paint to be used in week 5 isn't lemon or lime (2), cream (3) or white (4), so pale blue. Thus the lemon paint will be used in week 4 (2) and the lime paint in week 3. Week 4's job won't be the bedroom (1) or hallway (3), so the lounge. Week 3's job (lime, above) won't be the hallway (3), so the bedroom. Thus the kitchen will be painted in week 1 (3) and the hallway in week 2. The paint for the hallway is white.
**Thus:**
Week 1 - kitchen - cream;
Week 2 - hallway - white;
Week 3 - bedroom - lime;
Week 4 - lounge - lemon;
Week 5 - bathroom - pale blue.

## 115

The subject of the artist at easel No 1 wasn't the horse (clue 1), forest (clue 2) or mountain (3), so the dog. The subject chosen by the artist at No 2 wasn't the forest (2) or mountain (3), so the horse. Ronald was at No 1 (1) and the artist who used water-based paint was at No 3. Thus the artist who used pencils was at No 2 (2) and the forest was the subject of the artist at No 3. By elimination, the artist at No 4 painted the mountain, in oils (3), so the artist at No 1 used pastels. Harriet was at No 2 (3). Thelma wasn't at No 3 (1), so Charles was at No 3 and Thelma at No 4.

**Thus:**
Charles - easel No 3 - water-based - forest;
Harriet - easel No 2 - pencils - horse;
Ronald - easel No 1 - pastels - dog;
Thelma - easel No 4 - oils - mountain.

## 116

The Winter Fair wasn't in Regina (clue 2), Saskatoon (clue 3) or Edmonton (4), so Winnipeg where (3) she bought maps. The Autumn Fair was in Saskatoon (3). The $100 spend wasn't at the Autumn (3), Spring or Winter Fair (4), so at the Summer Fair. The Spring Fair was in Edmonton (4), so the Summer Fair was in Regina. The $400 spend wasn't at the Spring Fair (1), so (3) she spent $400 at the Autumn Fair and $200 at the Winter Fair. Thus $300 was spent at the Spring Fair and (1) kitchenware was at the Autumn Fair. Clothing wasn't at the Summer Fair (2), so at the Spring Fair. Paintings were bought at the Summer Fair.

**Thus:**
Spring - Edmonton - clothing - $300;
Summer - Regina - paintings - $100;
Autumn - Saskatoon - kitchenware - $400;
Winter - Winnipeg - maps - $200.

## 117

The race on planet E (furthest from the sun) isn't the Ermings (clue 1), Arinoms (clue 2), Brovides or Croptils (3), so the Dembles. The Croptils don't live on A or B (1) or D (3), so C. Thus Alpten is B (1) and the Ermings live on A. Planet A isn't Lanpet (2) or Entlap (3), so either Patnel or Naptle. Thus the Arinoms live on B (2) and Lanpet is C. By elimination, the Brovides live on D, so Entlap is E (3). Naptle isn't D (4), so A. Patnel is planet D.

**Thus:**
Planet A - Naptle - Ermings;
Planet B - Alpten - Arinoms;
Planet C - Lanpet - Croptils;
Planet D - Patnel - Brovides;
Planet E - Entlap - Dembles.

## 118

Remember throughout that each "new" picture contains parts of three "old" ones (intro). Rachel's brother's body is with her sister's legs (clue 2). Her mother's head and father's body are in the same picture (clue 1), but not with her brother's legs, so her aunt's legs. Rachel's brother's legs aren't with her mother's body (3), so her mother's body is with her father's legs. These aren't with her sister's head (3) and her sister's head isn't in the same picture as her brother's legs. Thus her sister's head is with her aunt's body and mother's legs. By elimination, her brother's legs are with her sister's body, and her brother's head is with her mother's body. Her father's head isn't with her sister's body (4), so her brother's body; and Rachel's sister's body is now with her aunt's head.

**Thus (head - body - legs):**
Aunt - sister - brother;
Brother - mother - father;
Father - brother - sister;
Mother - father - aunt;
Sister - aunt - mother.

## 119

The person who found WASP also found SPREE (clue 1) and the person who found WANE also found SWEEP (clue 2). The one who found SWAP also found WRAP (1) but not PREEN (with SEWN, 2), so NEWER. SEWN and PREEN (2) were thus also found by whoever found WARN. The person who found WARN isn't Neil (2), Mary or Peter (3), so Olivia. The person who found SNAP isn't Mary or Peter (4), so Neil. He didn't find SWEEP (2), so SPREE. By elimination, whoever found SPAN also found SWEEP. Peter didn't find WANE (3), so WRAP. Mary found WANE.

**Thus:**
Mary - SPAN - WANE - SWEEP;
Neil - SNAP - WASP - SPREE;
Olivia - SEWN - WARN - PREEN;
Peter - SWAP - WRAP - NEWER.

## 120

Naomi had been reading (clue 4), so Anna's DAUGHTER who had been painting (clue 2) is Alison. Naomi had an appointment to see the doctor (4). Corinne's child was taken to the hairdresser (3), so isn't Naomi. Nor is Corinne's child Mitch (3), so Barry. Alison's appointment was with her piano tutor (3), so Mitch's was with the optician. Mitch had been watching TV (1), so Barry was modelmaking. Naomi's mother isn't Mary (4), so Leonie. Mitch's mother is Mary.

**Thus:**
Alison - painting - Anna - piano tutor;
Barry - modelmaking - Corinne - hairdresser;
Mitch - watching TV - Mary - optician;
Naomi - reading - Leonie - doctor.

## 121

Rodney donated to the charity for sick animals (clue 1), Faith was collecting for war widows (clue 4)

# Solutions

and the collector for the charity for the blind was either Verity or Charity (5). Jimmy didn't donate to the charity for birds (2) and his sticker was sold by either Honor or Hope, so (by elimination) he supported the children's charity. Josephine didn't donate to the charity for the blind (3) or the war widows' charity (4), so Josephine's donation was to the bird's charity. Brian bought a sticker from Charity (5), so (by elimination), he supported the charity for the blind and Prudence gave to the one for the war widows. Rodney didn't buy a sticker from Honor or Verity (1), so Hope. Thus Jimmy bought a sticker from Honor (2) and Josephine's was from Verity.
**Thus:**
Brian - blind - Charity;
Jimmy - children - Honor;
Josephine - birds - Verity;
Prudence - war widows - Faith;
Rodney - animals - Hope.


## 122

The event which starts at 6.30 pm isn't on Thursday or Friday (clue 1), so the bowling is on Monday (clue 3) and Wednesday's event starts at 6.30 pm. The fashion show is on Tuesday. Friday's event isn't the movie trip (1) or dinner party (2), so the bridge party. The movie trip isn't on Thursday (1), so Wednesday, and Thursday's event is the dinner party. The bridge party starts at 7.30 pm (4) and the bowling at 6.45 pm. The fashion show starts at 7.15 pm (2) and the dinner party at 7.00 pm.
**Thus:**
Bowling - Monday - 6.45 pm;
Bridge party - Friday - 7.30 pm;
Dinner party - Thursday - 7.00 pm;
Fashion show - Tuesday - 7.15 pm;
Movie trip - Wednesday - 6.30 pm.


## 123

The 81-year-old woman isn't Beth (clue 2) or Noelle (clue 5), so Mary (4), and Leonie is 83. The 87-year-old man isn't Arthur (1) or Vince (5), so Lenny (6), and Richard is 85. Arthur and his wife are thus both 83 (1) and Vince is 84. Noelle is 86 (5), so Beth is 85. Since Leonie is 83 (above), her husband is Arthur, so Beth's (2) is Vince. Richard is 85 (above), so his wife is 81 (Mary, above) and Lenny's is Noelle.
**Thus (his age - her age):**
Arthur - Leonie - 83 - 83;
Lenny - Noelle - 87 - 86;
Richard - Mary - 85 - 81;
Vince - Beth - 84 - 85.


## 124

The 16-year-old isn't Myra (clue 1), Jill (clue 3) or Clarissa (4), so Penny. Her card wasn't from Ralph (1), Roger (2) or Rupert (3), so Reuben and (2) Roger

sent a card to the 17-year-old. Card D (furthest right) wasn't sent to Myra (1), Clarissa (4) or Penny (5), so Jill. Thus Rupert sent C (3) and Penny received B. Myra received A (1), so Clarissa received C. Myra is thus 20 (4), Clarissa is 19 and Jill is 17. Myra's card was sent by Ralph.
**Thus:**
Card A - Myra - Ralph - 20;
Card B - Penny - Reuben - 16;
Card C - Clarissa - Rupert - 19;
Card D - Jill - Roger - 17.


## 125

The person going to Australia has $800 (clue 2) and Lydia is going to Canada (clue 4). Hal has either $600 or $1,000 (1) and isn't going to the USA or New Zealand, so Singapore. Thus Hal has $1,000 (3) and Graham has $800. Frances has $600 (4) and Lydia has $300, so Nancy has $500. Nancy is going to New Zealand (1), so Frances is going to the USA.
**Thus:**
Frances - $600 - USA;
Graham - $800 - Australia;
Hal - $1,000 - Singapore;
Lydia - $300 - Canada;
Nancy - $500 - New Zealand.


## 126

The woman who paid $5.50 (most) isn't Roberta (clue 1), Nadine or Juliet (clue 3) or Verna (4), so Alison. The $3.50 (cheapest) egg wasn't in the yellow (1), gold (2), blue (3) or green box (4), so silver. It wasn't bought by Verna or Juliet (2) or Nadine (3), so by Roberta and (1) the egg in the yellow box cost $4.00. It wasn't bought by Verna (1) or Nadine (3), so by Juliet. The egg in the green box wasn't bought by Verna or Alison (4), so by Nadine. Verna paid $4.50 and Nadine $5.00 (4). Alison's egg was in the blue box (3), so Verna's was in the gold box.
**Thus:**
Alison - blue - $5.50;
Juliet - yellow - $4.00;
Nadine - green - $5.00;
Roberta - silver - $3.50;
Verna - gold - $4.50.


## 127

The tree with silver tinsel wasn't topped by a star or a Santa (clue 1) or a snowflake (clue 2), so an angel. The tree with a star on top was at either No 1 or No 3 (1), as was the one with the snowflake on top (2), so the tree with an angel/silver tinsel was at No 5 (1) and the one with a Santa on top was at No 7. Thus the one with a Santa on top had blue tinsel (2). Norman lives at No 5 (2) and the snowflake was on the tree at No 3, so the star was on the tree at No 1. Catherine

158

lives at either No 1 or No 3 (3) and Johnny at No 7. Catherine's tree didn't have gold tinsel (3), so purple. Lavinia lives at No 3 (4), so her tree was hung with gold tinsel and Catherine lives at No 1.

**Thus:**

Catherine - No 1 - purple - star;

Johnny - No 7 - blue - Santa;

Lavinia - No 3 - gold - snowflake;

Norman - No 5 - silver - angel.

## 128

Remember throughout that no more than one premium was paid per month (intro), as well as the fact that no-one paid car insurance in October, house insurance in August or life insurance in November (grid). The man who paid his car insurance in August isn't Gordon (clue 1), Leslie (clue 2) or Tim (4), so Henry. The man who paid his life insurance in December and (3) his house insurance in November isn't Gordon (1), Henry (2) or Leslie (4), so Tim. Tim paid his car insurance in September (1), Leslie paid his house insurance in October and Henry paid his house insurance in December (2), so Gordon paid his life insurance in September. Thus the man who paid his life insurance in September is Henry, so Gordon paid his life insurance in October and (1) his car insurance in November. By elimination, Henry paid his car insurance in August and Leslie paid his car insurance in December.

**Thus (car - house - life):**

Gordon - Nov - Sept - Oct;

Henry - Aug - Dec - Sept;

Leslie - Dec - Oct - Aug;

Tim - Sept - Nov - Dec.

## 129

Remember throughout that each "new" photo is made of three "old" photos (intro). Mr Ward's head has Mrs Fitt's body (clue 3). Miss Brown's head and Mr Neame's legs (clue 1) aren't with Mr Ward's body, so Mrs Moor's. Mr Ward's head/Mrs Fitt's body aren't with Miss Brown's legs (3), so Mrs Moor's. Mrs Moor's head has Mr Neame's body (2). Mrs Fitt's head isn't with Miss Brown's body (4), so Mr Ward's – thus (by elimination) they're with Miss Brown's legs. By elimination, Mr Neame's head is with Miss Brown's body which (4) isn't with Mrs Fitt's legs, so Mr Ward's. Mrs Moor's head is thus with Mrs Fitt's legs.

**Thus (head - body - legs):**

Miss Brown - Mrs Moor - Mr Neame;

Mrs Fitt - Mr Ward - Miss Brown;

Mrs Moor - Mr Neame - Mrs Fitt;

Mr Neame - Miss Brown - Mr Ward;

Mr Ward - Mrs Fitt - Mrs Moor.

## 130

Neil dressed as the monster (clue 1) and Moira as the witch (clue 2). The MAN (2) dressed as an Egyptian mummy wasn't James, so Callum. Tanya didn't go as the vampire (1), so as the ghost and James was the vampire. The fifth to arrive wasn't Neil or Tanya (1), Moira or Callum (2), so James. The first wasn't Neil (1), Moira (2) or Callum (3), so Tanya and (1) Neil was second. Moira arrived fourth (2) and Callum arrived third.

**Thus:**

Callum - third - mummy;

James - fifth - vampire;

Moira - fourth - witch;

Neil - second - monster;

Tanya - first - ghost.

## 131

The boy with 9 (most) pigs isn't Larry (clue 3), Malcolm (clue 5) or Trevor (6), so Andrew. Larry has either 7 or 9 cows (4), Andrew has 6 or 7 and Malcolm has 9 or 10 cows. Thus (2) Andrew isn't the boy with 14 (most). So the boy with 14 sheep has 6 cows (2) and 5 pigs. By elimination, he's Trevor. Andrew has 7 cows, Larry 9 (4) and Malcolm 10. The boy with 3 pigs has more sheep than Larry (1), so Larry has 7 pigs and Malcolm has 3. Malcolm has more sheep than Larry (1), but fewer than Andrew (5), so Malcolm has 10 sheep, Larry has 8 and Andrew has 12.

**Thus (cows - pigs - sheep):**

Andrew - 7 - 9 - 12;

Larry - 9 - 7 - 8;

Malcolm - 10 - 3 - 10;

Trevor - 6 - 5 - 14.

## 132

The poster bought in January isn't B (clue 1), A or D (clue 5), so C. Thus the *Way Out* poster is either B, C or D (4). Poster A isn't of a scene from *A Long Road* (2) or *Shivers* (5), so *Good Intentions*. The scene from *A Long Road* isn't on poster D (2), so Tommy Wayne isn't on C or D. Tommy Wayne isn't on A (3), so B. Liam Foster is on the poster next to and right of that bought in May. The scene from *Good Intentions* was bought in July (3), so D was bought in April. C features a scene from *A Long Road* (2). James Day is on D (1), so Mike Poole is on A. B doesn't show a scene from *Way Out* (4), so *Shivers,* and *Way Out* is featured on D.

**Thus:**

Poster A - Mike Poole - *Good Intentions* - July;

Poster B - Tommy Wayne - *Shivers* - May;

Poster C - Liam Foster - *A Long Road* - January;

Poster D - James Day - *Way Out* - April.

# Solutions

**133**

George went on the ride either 3 or 4 times (clue 1), as did Olga (clue 2), and Helen went on either 6 or 7 times. Either the child whose preferred ride was the merry-go-round went on 5 times and the one whose preferred ride was the bumper cars went on 6 times (1) or the child whose preferred ride was the merry-go-round went on 6 times and the one whose preferred ride was the bumper cars went on 7 times. Thus the preferred ride of whoever went on 6 times was either the merry-go-round or the bumper cars. Thus Bill whose preferred ride was the ferris wheel (3) went on 5 times and whoever preferred the pirate boat went on 4 times. By elimination, the child whose preferred ride was the big dipper went on 3 times, the one whose preferred ride was the merry-go-round went on 6 times (1) and the one whose preferred ride was the bumper cars went on 4 times (1), so Olga 3 times (2) and Helen 6. Clara went on 7 times.

**Thus:**

Bill - ferris wheel - 5 times;

Clara - bumper cars - 7 times;

George - pirate boat - 4 times;

Helen - merry-go-round - 6 times;

Olga - big dipper - 3 times.